Brevity

Brevity

The Art of Writing Very Short Fiction

A Guide to Writing Flash Fiction

A Short Short-Short Primer

A Flash Fiction Handbook

David Galef

COLUMBIA UNIVERSITY PRESS   NEW YORK

COLUMBIA UNIVERSITY PRESS
Publishers Since 1893
New York   Chichester, West Sussex

cup.columbia.edu

Library of Congress Cataloging-in-Publication Data

Names: Galef, David, author.
Title: Brevity : a flash fiction handbook / David Galef.
Description: New York : Columbia University Press, 2016. | Includes bibliographical
    references and index.
Identifiers: LCCN 2016019207 (print) | LCCN 2016032149 (ebook) |
    ISBN 9780231179683 (cloth : alk. paper) | ISBN 9780231179690 (pbk. : alk. paper) |
    ISBN 9780231543132 (e-book)
Subjects: LCSH: Flash fiction—Authorship. | Flash fiction—Technique.
Classification: LCC PN3377.5.F53 G35 2016 (print) | LCC PN3377.5.F53 (ebook) |
    DDC 808.3/1—dc23
LC record available at https://lccn.loc.gov/2016019207

Columbia University Press books are printed on permanent and durable acid-free paper.
Printed in the United States of America

COVER AND BOOK DESIGN BY VIN DANG
COVER PHOTOGRAPH BY ALEXIA GALATI

Contents

Acknowledgments

THE WRITING OF A BOOK LIKE THIS involves a lot of people. I'd like to thank all the contributing writers in these pages, authors whose work shows how much you can do in a small space. I'm also grateful to the staff at Columbia University Press, especially Philip Leventhal and Justine Evans, without whose support this textbook might never have seen print. Colleagues of mine at Montclair State University, namely, Lee Behlman, Caroline Dadas, Jon Greenberg, Emily Isaacs, Naomi Liebler, and Jeffrey Miller, made valuable suggestions during a campus presentation on flash fiction. Manuscript readers to whom I'm indebted include Eileen Pollack, Michael Martone, and Fred Leebron. Many in the flash fiction anthology business were kind enough to provide tips, particularly that inveterate editing duo James Thomas and Robert Shapard, shepherds of the *Sudden Fiction* series, also Tara Masih, coeditor of *Best Small Fictions*; Tara Laskowski at *SmokeLong Quarterly*; Robert Swartwood of *Hint Fiction*; Tom Hazuka and Mark Budman, longtime editors of flash fiction collections of many stripes; Abigail Beckel and Kathleen Rooney of Rose Metal Press; and Erin McKnight at Queen's Ferry Press. The translator Margaret Jull Costa provided advice about Spanish translations.

I'm especially grateful to my wife, Beth Weinhouse, who, despite her busy schedule, always made time to look at a few pages or listen to me perorate. I'm also in debt to my son, Daniel Galef, an astute reader and writer who helped with everything from fiction selections to tracking down authors in their electronic lairs.

A Short Introduction

WHAT'S USUALLY UNDER 1,500 WORDS, feels like a short story, and is read all over?

Flash fiction.

Several decades ago, flash fiction pieces were known as short-shorts, sometimes confused with an item of clothing that came to midthigh or higher. More recently, flash fiction, once used to label anything even briefer than a short-short, has become the catchall term for any minuscule narrative. The results can be provocative, amusing, hard-hitting, or enigmatic. Does size matter? Paradoxically, leaving out material can make a piece of fiction feel more expansive. Good flash fiction often relies on the art of implication rather than statement, depending on suggestions that lead to a large, unspoken whole. This idea is what Robert Browning alludes to in his poem on the Renaissance painter Andrea del Sarto when he writes "less is more." Flash fiction may also be compressed, and with pressure comes intensity, another reason that flash fiction has won so many fans. As one reader described it, "It's like someone's telling me an urgent message, and I'd better listen." A good piece of flash fiction doesn't just exist; it happens. It has, in the words of one fiction-workshop participant, "the immediacy of a newsfeed."

Yet flash fiction has been around since the beginning of fiction, especially if you include short narrative lyrics, Aesop's fables, and biblical stories. Sei Shōnagon's *Pillow Book* from 11th-century Japan features short sketches that could qualify, as does the 14th-century Italian *Decameron*, by Boccaccio. American authors including Edgar Alan Poe and Ernest Hemingway dabbled in the form, and during the golden age of the American short story, from the 1920s through the 1950s, flash fiction flourished here and there. I have on my bookshelf a volume entitled *The Best Short Shorts of 1932*, edited by Paul Ernest Anderson and Lionel White and published by G. P. Putnam's & Sons, as well as the *Anthology of Best Original Short-Shorts* series inaugurated by Robert Oberfirst in the 1950s.

But the form didn't truly achieve critical mass until Robert Shapard and James Thomas's anthology *Sudden Fiction* in 1986. There, under the banner of the new, were seventy narratives ranging from one to five pages. Because of their quick impact, the original term was *blasters*, and the title *Sudden Fiction* carried from anthology to anthology in a growing series. Yet the name "short-shorts" stuck, from the first anthology's subtitle, *American Short-Short Stories*. Fiction workshops embraced the form, and it began to spread. As the form proliferated, it began to spawn smaller versions: flash fiction, which achieved its effects in about 500–1,000 words, and microfiction, which did the same in 250–500 words (though these limits were hardly universally agreed on).

What's the limit of vanishing returns? A magazine called *NFG* some years ago ran a fiction contest that restricted all entries to 69 words, and 55 is another formula that's been tried. A recent Norton anthology, edited by Robert Swartwood and Natalie McNabb, is called *Hint Fiction: An Anthology of Stories in 25 Words or Fewer*. These days, you can see a lot on the Web, including two-sentence horror stories and nanofiction, also known as Twitter fiction or Twiction, weighing in at only 140 characters, including punctuation and blank spaces.

Hemingway is famous for supposedly constructing a short story in six words: "For sale: baby shoes, never worn." The boast is probably apocryphal (Hemingway scholars have been unable to find any record of it), but the story remains in wide currency. The image is poignant and haunting because it is incomplete: Are the shoes being sold because the infant died, or was the original purchase based on a hoped-for event that never happened? What do the shoes look like, who's selling them, and in what state of mind? For everything left out, an image or narrative segment comes to mind.

What's the point? you might ask. Or: *What's left?* The point is not just to cram as much as possible into a line, though practicing the art of economy is always useful. Making a few words stand in for a whole is a powerful effect that any good poet knows: all summer in a day, or the universe in a grain of sand. A microcosm may stand in for a macrocosm: a beehive may signify the rise of an advanced civilization. It's all a matter of representation, which is in fact a good definition of art. We might even call flash fiction "concentrated story."

If art is life with the boring parts left out, as more than one commentator has quipped, short-shorts are both artful and artistic. The rest of this handbook is devoted to demonstrating this point in many different forms. The chapters include close looks at vignettes, twist stories, what-if premises, fables . . . everything from anecdotes to the vanishing point of narrative.

More specifically, the first series of chapters focuses on forms that are particularly successful in miniature, such as character sketches and diary entries, prose poems and list-stories. A section on how to pare down material marks the midpoint. After that come chapters on certain techniques or treatments that work well when applied to a small space, such as surrealism and metafiction, mass compression and the simple opposition of two viewpoints.

In addition, each chapter concludes with exercises or prompts designed to get readers writing. Two sample stories at the end of each chapter are useful as models and for analysis, with discussion questions. Instructors should find this textbook appropriate for almost any course devoted to the art of fiction, and the anticipated readership ranges from creative writing students in a classroom to the larger realm of writers who want to improve their craft. Writing so that every word counts makes for powerful, memorable work. Those who read this book with attention and work through the exercises will be rewarded with demonstrably greater competency and probably a few noteworthy pieces of their own.

Enough preamble. The aesthetics of the miniature world depend on economy and efficiency. To that end, here are some starting tips:

Cut the opening, and get right to the point.

Focus on the one telling detail, not a full description.

Don't "conclude," but instead end with an action or an image.

This is apt advice for any good fiction, but particularly true when working in a tight space. Now let's get started.

Brevity

Vignettes

BY DEFINITION, flash fiction is rendered in miniature. But what happens when you start cutting down on words? What becomes of plot, character development, and thematic depth? Obviously, some of what you can attain in a longer story is going to have to go. Forget the long landscape description or the three scenes showing the grandmother's slow decay from Parkinson's. On the other hand, some treatments are particularly suited for the short run. One well-known form is the vignette.

The vignette started in 15th-century printing as a decorative border of vines around a page, then turned into what the vines enclosed, usually a page with an illustration. We now think of it as an illustrative scene, a literary sketch. The French coined a term for this form, calling it *tranche de vie* (literally, "slice of life"), and its ingenuity lies in what any cross-section reveals: the hidden depths of an interior view.

Picture two eight-year-olds playing croquet: those unwieldy mallets, the lawn sloping unfairly, and one ball headed for the bushes. This vignette, just begun, might be called "Game." It shows the seemingly innocent fun had by two small children on a Sunday afternoon, with more than a hint of sibling rivalry. We'll name the children Ivan and

Sandra and make them neighbors. You can hear the smack of mallets on the balls along with some conversation about school. But after the first paragraph, Ivan says something nasty about Sandra's mother. Sandra responds not by hitting Ivan's ball with hers but by kicking it. The "game" escalates from there.

As you can see, "Game" isn't a proper story with a beginning, middle, and end. It's a moving picture that becomes a sketch or scene, suggesting something beyond. The term "sketch" is all the more apt when you think of visual art, in which a sketch is the essential lines of a drawing, but not filled in. Here are some guidelines for creating a vignette:

Focus on a moment. If you start to chronicle any substantial period, stop, and instead deepen the presentation of what's already there: waiting half an hour for a date to show up, a missed opportunity to help a stranger.

Develop only as much as you need to register an impression of either a character or an event or even a mood. One trait indicates a sunny personality; a distorted shadow indicates trouble.

Think in psychological terms. Your sketch has a meaning beyond its mere existence because of what it represents: an old woman who can't enjoy a summer afternoon, a boss who won't take no for an answer. Here are five pointers for this kind of treatment:

1 Don't merely describe. Follow the action. Dramatize.
2 Do more with less. One short scene from a day is plenty.
3 Be representative. This part that you're illustrating can stand in for a whole life.
4 Go for evocative, concrete details, not abstractions.
5 If possible, find a way to give shadows and depth to your sketch. Make it mean more than what it seems on the surface.

One of the best practitioners of the vignette is the French author Colette, who wrote searching portraits of love and relationships. Take a look at "The Other Wife," in which Marc is having lunch with his new wife, Alice, at an elegant restaurant when he spots his previous wife at a nearby table. Yet the focus is mainly on the dynamic between Alice and Marc: he dictates where they sit and what they order; he comments on how much weight Alice is putting on. Any author could go on in this vein, but Colette won't. She doesn't need to. She makes her point through gestures, descriptions, and tone. Marc is older than Alice, "his thick hair, threaded here and there with white silk." He dominates, yet nonchalantly, as if always used to getting his way. In which case, who is this woman at the other table, who somehow escaped his grasp? The few details are both alluring and enigmatic: "The woman in white, whose smooth, lustrous hair reflected the light from the sea in azure patches, was smoking a cigarette with her eyes half closed" (translated by Matthew Ward). If this woman, who seems so self-assured, rejected Marc, what does that imply about the prospects for the new marriage? For the first time, Alice entertains doubts about what she's embarked upon. The end is suggestive rather than conclusive: here is a part to suggest the whole. With good vignettes, that's all you need. The complete story is printed in "Readings."

EXERCISES

❶ Think of yesterday as a sequence of events, then choose a common incident, such as lunch, an hour at work, or a car ride. Now describe it, animate it, and dramatize it so that the reader gets a vivid picture of what's happening, on both an exterior and an interior level. For instance: With a smile, I serve plate after plate of the daily special, spaghetti and meatballs, at Abe's Diner, but I really hate my job. Or: She hitches a ride home with a coworker, a man she'd like to ask out, but she hasn't got the nerve. What incident did you choose, what did it show, and why was it significant? How much of the character did you reveal, and in what ways? Did anything change over the course of the event?

❷ Here are some specific directives: What slice of life, the more ordinary, the better, would you use to show envy at the way your parents treat your brother? How good does your friend think she is at driving versus how inept she really is? Why is that man on the curb accosting passersby by asking the same question over and over?

READINGS

Colette: "The Other Wife"

TRANSLATED BY MATTHEW WARD

"Table for two? This way, Monsieur, Madame, there is still a table next to the window, if Madame and Monsieur would like a view of the bay."

Alice followed the maitre d'.

"Oh, yes. Come on, Marc, it'll be like having lunch on a boat on the water . . ."

Her husband caught her by passing his arm under hers. "We'll be more comfortable over there."

"There? In the middle of all those people? I'd much rather . . ."

"Alice, please."

He tightened his grip in such a meaningful way that she turned around. "What's the matter?"

"Shh . . ." he said softly, looking at her intently, and led her toward the table in the middle.

"What is it, Marc?"

"I'll tell you, darling. Let me order lunch first. Would you like the shrimp? Or the eggs in aspic?"

"Whatever you like, you know that."

They smiled at one another, wasting the precious time of an overworked maitre d', stricken with a kind of nervous dance, who was standing next to them, perspiring.

"The shrimp," said Marc. "Then the eggs and bacon. And the cold chicken with a romaine salad. *Fromage blanc*? The house specialty? We'll go with the specialty. Two strong coffees. My chauffeur will be having lunch also, we'll be leaving again at two o'clock. Some cider? No, I don't trust it . . . Dry champagne."

He sighed as if he had just moved an armoire, gazed at the colorless midday sea, at the pearly white sky, then at his wife, whom he found lovely in her little Mercury hat with its large, hanging veil.

"You're looking well, darling. And all this blue water makes your eyes look green, imagine that! And you've put on weight since you've been traveling . . . It's nice up to a point, but only up to a point!"

Her firm, round breasts rose proudly as she leaned over the table.

"Why did you keep me from taking that place next to the window?"

Marc Seguy never considered lying. "Because you were about to sit next to someone I know."

"Someone I don't know?"

"My ex-wife."

She couldn't think of anything to say and opened her blue eyes wider.

"So what, darling? It'll happen again. It's not important."

The words came back to Alice and she asked, in order, the inevitable questions. "Did she see you? Could she see that you saw her? Will you point her out to me?"

"Don't look now, please, she must be watching us . . . The lady with brown hair, no hat, she must be staying in this hotel. By herself, behind those children in red . . ."

"Yes. I see."

Hidden behind some broad-brimmed beach hats, Alice was able to look at the woman who, fifteen months ago, had still been her husband's wife.

"Incompatibility," Marc said. "Oh, I mean . . . total incompatibility! We divorced like well-bred people, almost like friends, quietly, quickly. And then I fell in love with you, and you really wanted to be happy with me. How lucky we are that our happiness doesn't involve any guilty parties or victims!"

The woman in white, whose smooth, lustrous hair reflected the light from the sea in azure patches, was smoking a cigarette with her eyes half closed. Alice turned back toward her husband, took some shrimp and butter, and ate calmly. After a moment's silence she asked: "Why didn't you ever tell me that she had blue eyes, too?"

"Well, I never thought about it!"

He kissed the hand she was extending toward the bread basket and she blushed with pleasure. Dusky and ample, she might have seemed somewhat coarse, but the changeable blue of her eyes and her wavy, golden hair made her look like a frail and sentimental blonde. She vowed overwhelming gratitude to her husband. Immodest without knowing it, everything about her bore the overly conspicuous marks of extreme happiness.

They ate and drank heartily, and each thought the other had forgotten the woman in white. Now and then, however, Alice laughed too loudly, and Marc was careful about his posture, holding his shoulders back, his head up. They waited quite a long time for their coffee, in silence. An incandescent river, the straggled reflection of the invisible sun overhead, shifted slowly across the sea and shone with a blinding brilliance.

"She's still there, you know," Alice whispered.

"Is she making you uncomfortable? Would you like to have coffee somewhere else?"

"No, not at all! She's the one who must be uncomfortable! Besides, she doesn't exactly seem to be having a wild time, if you could see her . . ."

"I don't have to. I know that look of hers."

"Oh, was she like that?"

He exhaled his cigarette smoke through his nostrils and knitted his eyebrows. "Like that? No. To tell you honestly, she wasn't happy with me."

"Oh, really now!"

"The way you indulge me is so charming, darling . . . It's crazy . . . You're an angel . . . You love me . . . I'm so proud when I see those eyes of yours. Yes, those eyes . . . She . . . I just didn't know how to make her happy, that's all. I didn't know how."

"She's just difficult!"

Alice fanned herself irritably, and cast brief glances at the woman in white, who was smoking, her head resting against the back of the cane chair, her eyes closed with an air of satisfied lassitude.

Marc shrugged his shoulders modestly.

"That's the right word," he admitted. "What can you do? You have to feel sorry for people who are never satisfied. But we're satisfied . . . Aren't we, darling?"

She did not answer. She was looking furtively, and closely, at her husband's face, ruddy and regular; at his thick hair, threaded here and there with white silk; at his short, well-cared-for hands; and doubtful for the first time, she asked herself, "What more did she want from him?"

And as they were leaving, while Marc was paying the bill and asking for the chauffeur and about the route, she kept looking, with envy and curiosity, at the woman in white, this dissatisfied, this difficult, this superior . . .

(998 WORDS)

DISCUSSION

One aim of a good vignette is to set down the details so that the reader can predict a bit of the future. What will happen between Marc and his new wife? What could occur to disrupt the pattern? Write a vignette about Marc and a third wife.

Isaac Babel: "An Incident on the Nevsky Prospekt"
TRANSLATED BY PETER CONSTANTINE

I turn from the Liteiny Prospekt onto the Nevsky Prospekt. In front of me walks a young, one-armed man, swaying. He is in uniform. His empty sleeve is pinned to the black cloth of his jacket.

The young man sways. He looks cheerful to me. It is three in the afternoon. Soldiers are selling lilies of the valley, and generals are selling chocolate. It is spring, warm, bright.

I had been mistaken, the one-armed man is not cheerful. He walks up to the wooden fence, which is brightly decorated with posters, and sits down on the hot asphalt of the sidewalk. His body slides down, saliva dribbles out of his distorted mouth, his head, narrow and yellow, lolls to the side.

Slowly people start gathering. They have gathered. We stand there sluggish, whispering, eyeing each other with dull, dumbfounded eyes.

A golden-haired lady is quicker than the rest. She is wearing a wig, has light-blue eyes, bluish cheeks, a powdered nose, and bouncing false teeth. She has fully grasped the situation: the poor invalid has fainted from hunger after returning from a German prison camp.

Her blue cheeks bob up and down. "Ladies and gentlemen!" she says. "The Germans are filling the streets of our capital with their cigar smoke while our poor martyrs . . ."

We all gather around the outstretched body in an unhurried but attentive herd. We are all touched by the lady's words.

Prostitutes drop little sugar cubes into the soldier's cap with anxious haste, a Jew buys potato pancakes from a stand, a foreigner throws a bright stream of new ten-kopeck coins, a young lady from one of the stores brings out a cup of coffee.

The invalid writhes on the asphalt, drinks the coffee from the Chinese cup, and chews sweet pies.

"Like a beggar on a church porch!" he mutters, hiccuping, his cheeks flooding with bright tears. "Just like a beggar, just like they've all come to a circus, my God!"

The lady asks us to go on our way. She asks us to show some tact. The invalid rolls onto his side. His stretched-out leg pops up into the air like the leg of a toy clown.

At that moment a carriage pulls up at the curb. A sailor climbs out, followed by a blue-eyed girl with white stockings and suede shoes. She is pressing an armful of flowers to her breast.

The sailor stands in front of the wooden fence, his legs apart. The invalid raises his limp neck and peers timidly at the sailor's bare neck, his carefully curled hair, and his drunk and joyful face covered with specks of powder.

The sailor slowly takes out his wallet and throws a forty-ruble note into the hat. The young man scrapes it up with his rigid, black fingers and raises his watery, canine eyes to the sailor.

The sailor sways on his long legs, takes a step backward, and winks slyly and tenderly at the soldier on the ground.

Stripes of flame light up the sky. An idiot's smile stretches the soldier's lips, we hear a wheezing, yowling laugh, and a stifling stench of alcohol pours from his mouth.

"Lie where you are, Comrade," the sailor tells him, "lie where you are!"

It is spring on the Nevsky Prospekt, warm, bright. The sailor's wide back slowly recedes. The blue-eyed girl, leaning against his round shoulder, smiles quietly. The cripple, wriggling on the asphalt, is overcome by an abrupt, joyous, and nonsensical fit of laughter.

(584 WORDS)

DISCUSSION

What exactly is the plight of the one-armed young man? What does the I-narrator notice—and ignore? Put a different victim in the same place.

Character Sketches

THE WRITER ANNE LAMOTT has described how character in fiction develops slowly, like a Polaroid picture, but flash fiction doesn't usually proceed at that pace. To some extent, the impression of character in brief depictions mimics reality: no one hands you a thick dossier on the person you're about to see; rather, you catch a glimpse of a teenager on a skateboard with a red-and-white-striped scarf—and then you lose sight of her behind the bridge. Or you sit in a library carrel across from a rheumy-eyed gentleman who keeps clearing his throat. Unless you happen to strike up a conversation, that's all you know.

Maybe a few beguiling details are all that's necessary. Never mind the plot; focus on the individual. For many readers, that's what matters most. In a character portrait, you can do without any specific action and just focus on noticeable aspects: his sweaty hands, her big feet, his way of eating hamburgers in a circling maneuver, or hers of peeling fruit with a knife and fork. They can be physical or psychological attributes, habits, employment, or even bits of the past or future: "Five years from now, Karla will have a three-month love affair with the paralegal at her law office."

Whatever details you choose, make them count in a pattern: Richard's collection of harmonicas makes people think he's musical, though he can't even carry a tune—which is odd because he lives with a blues guitar player. In his dreams, he performs onstage in front of huge crowds, playing all 73 of his instruments.

A character sketch is just that: a sketch. It's not a filled-in portrait but an outline, a suggestive pattern, a line on a graph from which the reader can extrapolate. You can cram your small space with details in seventeen different directions, but unless you're veering toward parody, you're probably better off with the flash fiction principle of pared-down representation. Stick to one or two defining traits and their implications. They needn't be big and important, just salient—and not abstract. Don't say that Alex is a good cook; say that his veal piccata has just the right amount of lemon. Sure, Elizabeth is tall, but a better visual clue for readers is that she can dust the top of the refrigerator without reaching for the step stool.

Don't like static portraits? Bear in mind that character is potential action. Henry James in "The Art of Fiction" famously declared, "What is character but the determination of incident? What is incident but the illustration of character?" If you have two women in a bar, both in love with Tom, and then Tom shows up, you've put together a conflict that may blow up during the first round of gin and tonics. Or: a man desperately wants to stay sober, but the woman he loves is an alcoholic who craves similar-minded company. So how much does he love her? Given appropriate character description, the reader can imagine a future.

Also, character sketches don't have to be merely description. Dynamic characters *move*, physically or psychologically. Look at the way he fidgets at the back of his night class in accounting. What's he got in his knapsack? By the end of your flash fiction that character may have changed his ambitions or at least be on the road to something new, even if it's only a different way of thinking. Raymond Carver once wrote a short piece called "Fat," in which a hefty man at a restaurant, through his huge appetite, influences a waitress to expect more from life. The portrait may not seem like it amounts to much. But it does.

EXERCISES

❶ Assign a character one salient trait, from a big, misshapen chin to a habit of counting steps on the walk to the bus. Where does that feature lead to?

❷ Present a character who's more than the sum of her parts or a character who's more than one character.

READINGS

L. E. Leone: "The Argument for a Shotgun"

You wake up in the middle of the night afraid of what? For me it's dead chickens, no more eggs and a bloodless bloody mess to clean. Weasels'll wipe out a whole houseload of chickens in one night, only knocking off the heads and sucking out the brains. For example.

For example I dream a fox with wirecutters and a crowbar.

"Where are you going?" asks my wife.

"Bathroom," I say.

"Why are you putting on your hat? Why are you putting on your shoes?"

"Go back to sleep," I say.

In the bathroom I open the window and stick my head all the way out into northern California, middle of the night. I think I hear a scratching sound coming from the vicinity of the chicken house. Bobcat, I think, trying to dig its way under the fence.

I need a shotgun. I really should have a shotgun, I think, running outside to meet the enemy with a curling iron and a toilet-bowl brush.

The enemy, this time, is fog, condensing into water droplets on oak tree leaves and dripping onto other oak tree leaves, dripping down all the way eventually into the dead, crispy stuff I never rake around the chicken run. I stand there under the tree in the dark until my eyes adjust to no bobcats, no foxes, no hungry eyes or glistening teeth; just fog, just watery particles of atmosphere, the is of what isn't, suspended like berries all around me—visible only because up there somewhere there's a moon.

I stand where I am until my heartrate returns to normal. Then I brandish the toilet-bowl brush, stab at the fog with the curling iron, and head back inside.

"What was it?" my wife asks.

"Nothing," I say.

(292 WORDS)

DISCUSSION

What bothers the narrator? What kind of man would you say he is? Would his wife agree? Write what's going to happen next.

Josefina Estrada: "The Extravagant Behavior of the Naked Woman"
TRANSLATED BY MARGARET JULL COSTA

The woman who walks naked through the streets of Santa María provokes astonishment in the children, delight in the men, and incredulity and anger in the women. She sits down at the corner of Sor Juana Inés de la Cruz and Sabino, next to the bicycle repair shop. The children come out of the two adjacent slums and cross the street to watch her as she sniffs glue from a bag, her only possession. She doesn't seem to care that she's naked, yet neither could you say that she'd made a conscious decision to display her dark, abundant flesh.

Even when she's sitting down you can tell she's a woman of vast stature. At shoulder level, her hair is a mass of tangles that contain balls of chewing gum, bits of earth, dust and fluff. The applause and whistles of the onlookers grow louder when she opens her legs and begins to scratch herself hard in the most impenetrable part of her being. At this point, the young men, who are always hanging around, can't suppress their laughter. Instinctively, as if fearing that at any moment they too might reveal their mysteries, they finger the flies of their trousers.

And when the woman lies down and turns her back on them, the onlookers begin throwing things at her. She takes a while to react, but they all know that as soon as she sits up, she'll get to her feet and chase her attackers. And the children will then be able to see that her breasts are not, in fact, stuck fast to her ample abdomen. Some of the smaller children go and tell their mothers that "the woman who wears no underpants or anything" is on the loose again. And their mothers forbid them to go back outside.

There was a period when she was seen by several women near where Aldama crosses Mina. Then for two years she prowled up and down Avenida Guerrero. She would go to sleep surrounded by a pile of clothes donated by well-meaning people, and which served her as both pillow and mattress. When she grew tired of her bundle of clothes, she would burn it using the same solvent she inhaled.

The huge, dark woman goes into building sites to wash. The glee of the workers reaches its height when she bends over to drink from the tap. They're beside themselves when she picks up handfuls of lime and powders her armpits. Any man bold enough to approach her has always been repelled by the ferocity of her insults. The women who live around Calle Sor Juana complain not about the exhibition she makes of herself but about the fact that she's freer than the men. Instead of putting an end to the extravagant behavior of this woman—which arouses lewd thoughts even in the most saintly of men—the police, they say, spend all their time arresting drunks.

(484 WORDS)

DISCUSSION

If the naked woman were clothed, would she still be objectionable? What's salient about this character? Is her size an issue? Her attitude? Or are other people the problem? Note how a character sketch often pulls in other characters, if only by implication.

Letters

A LETTER TO SOMEONE IS ALSO CALLED AN EPISTLE, and epistolary fiction presents a story in one or more letters. The form is as old as the letter itself. In the 12th century, the affair between the French philosopher Pierre Abélard and Héloïse d'Argenteuil was immortalized in their copious exchange of letters. Around the time of the 18th century, entire epistolary novels sprang up. Letters that convey more than news, that enact events in a narrative mode, can be as exciting as any short story. The form endures even as e-mail and texting have supplanted ink and paper. Fiction in the form of letters features one person addressing another but with the formal barrier of written words. What restrictions does this medium impose? Some items that you wouldn't say out loud, you can confide in a private letter: your suspicions that your brother is trying to kill you, expressed to your father, who might not be swayed by a mere conversation. Oppositely, some material you might whisper into someone's ear—"I love you"—but wouldn't want to commit to on paper, so you write around the topic: "You strike me as the kind of person whose company I always enjoy . . ." Thus, a story written in letters may be intimate yet distanced, revealing yet only through insinuation. Epistolary works offer the satisfaction of a letter in the mail: news from outside, a breath of fresh paper, a message containing anything from family updates to personal crises.

But letters may be no more than a paragraph or even a few lines, a trend toward brevity accentuated in our electronic age. (For transcripts of telephone calls and Skyping, see the chapter "Two Viewpoints.") A traditional epistolary flash fiction might consist of several brief letters between two friends, one of whom attended the second wedding of an old teacher while the other one stayed away out of embarrassment—the twenty-year-old memory of a bad grade. But with current technology, it could also be devoted to the text messages between two friends, one of whom is already at the wedding while the other is still en route, stuck in the back of a taxi. Since this is flash fiction, you may have space for only one exchange of letters or a short ping-pong game of texts, but that should be enough to focus on one incident or a single argument that reveals volumes (or many kilobytes' worth of data). What is the one point that you wish to convey to "Dear So-and-So"? Conversely, what prompts the texting to build to a flurry or die down to the emoticon :(?

Given a short space, have your letter or letters focus on only one idea or event. Brevity and focus will build intensity. Whatever the means of communication, the point of some letters is to deliver a point of view or argument. Let's say the letter writer is worried that his new tutoring agency will flop: not enough families in Hackettown seem to care about academic achievement, or maybe they just don't know how much she can help their kids or don't care to pay for it. He makes a little joke about second-rate education in First World nations. How well does he know the recipient? He addresses her as "Liz" and includes a comment about the woman's son, in the fourth grade at Foxton. He commiserates with her over her duties as the new head of the PTA there: power, yes, but all that responsibility and so many decisions to make! By the end of the letter, it's clear what the letter writer wants, a recommendation for his tutoring agency, coming from the head of the PTA. Perhaps the last sentence hints at what he can provide in return—something to do with the woman's son, who's doing horribly in math?

Letters are convenient vehicles for exposition, though innuendo and allusion may cloak the facts. Why does this woman address her coworker as "dude"? What is she alluding to when she refers to "that exciting incident in your office"? Would she say something like that out loud? Think hard about what people put in a letter that they wouldn't say in conversation and vice versa. This license extends to e-mail, in which people type stuff they'd never dream of speaking.

Don't neglect salutations and closings, as well as terms of address. "Dear, dear Bruce" is a world apart from "Bruce" with a colon afterward. "Love" is almost perfunctory, compared to "Love always." What's a new variation on "xo"? How can you smuggle in information that both parties know (and so wouldn't detail much) but that the reader otherwise doesn't have a clue about: the specifics behind a sexual harassment case; the particulars of a lousy film that they saw together; the $500 that one owes the other but that would be impolite to mention directly?

Finally: feel free to push the limits of letter writing. That includes three P.S. notes, writing in the margins, or whatever the bounds of your cyberspace include.

EXERCISES

❶ Write a letter of apology to a former friend, or demonstrate how that former friend might write to you. What exactly are you sorry for, or are you not really regretful and just being polite? Anchor the feeling in a recalled incident. Could the letter betray annoyance that you feel obliged to write at all? Are you aware of that resentment, or is it unconscious?

❷ Piece together a series of flash-mob texts—gone very wrong. What was the intent behind the gathering? What was the damage, and is it correctable with more texts?

READINGS

Yasunari Kawabata: "Canaries"

TRANSLATED BY J. MARTIN HOLMAN

Madam:

I must break my promise and write a letter to you just one more time. I can no longer keep the canaries I received from you last year. My wife always cared for them. My only function was to look at them—to think of you when I saw them.

You were the one who said it, weren't you? "You have a wife and I have a husband. Let's stop seeing each other. If only you didn't have a wife. I am giving you these canaries to remember me by. Look at them. These canaries are a couple now, but the shopkeeper simply caught a male and female at random and put them in a cage. The canaries themselves had nothing to do with it. Anyway, please remember me with these birds. Perhaps it's odd to give living creatures as a souvenir, but our memories, too, are alive. Someday the canaries will die. And, when the time comes that the memories between us must die, let them die."

Now the canaries look as though they are about to die. The one who kept them has died. A painter like me, negligent and poor as I am, cannot keep such frail birds. I'll put it plainly. My wife used to care for the birds, and now she is dead. Since my wife has died, I wonder if the birds will also die. And so, madam, was it my wife who brought me memories of you?

I considered setting the canaries free, but, since my wife's death, the birds' wings appear to have suddenly grown weak. Besides, these birds don't know the sky. The pair has no companions in the city or woods nearby with whom they could flock. And if one of them were to fly off alone, they would each die separately. But, then, you *did* say that the man at the pet shop had merely caught one male and one female at random and put them in a cage.

Speaking of which, I don't want to sell them back to a bird dealer because you gave these birds to me. And I don't want to return them to you either, since my wife was the one who cared for them. Besides, these birds—which you had probably already forgotten—would be a lot of trouble for you.

I'll say it again. It was because my wife was here that the birds have lived until now—serving as a memory of you. So, madam, I want to have the canaries follow her in death. Keeping my memories of you alive was not the only thing my wife did. How was I able to have loved a woman like you? Wasn't it because my wife remained with me? My wife made me forget all the pain in my life. She avoided seeing the other half of my life. Had she not done so, I would surely have averted my eyes or cast down my gaze before a woman like you.

Madam, it's all right, isn't it, if I kill the canaries and bury them in my wife's grave?

(514 WORDS)

DISCUSSION

In what terms does the letter writer compare his wife and the woman with whom he's had an affair? What might the letter writer say to the woman if he were in the same room as her? Note that he doesn't seem to blame himself in the least. What might be the woman's response?

Phil Karasik: "Mickey the Dog Phones Home"

Hey, it's me . . . your dog, Mickey. I'm sorry I haven't called. Soooo, yeah, I'm just gonna say it. I'm in a little bit of a bind. I met this bitch a few weeks ago and, uh, you know, she was digging my rap and whatnot. So I brought her back to the house for a couple of drinks and well, one thing led to another and, so, here's the deal: she hits me up by text the other day and says she's late, you know, and that they're mine.

Dude, I kinda freaked. I mean, I just needed some space. Some time to clear my head. So, I had to jet for awhile. I didn't even know where to go or what to do. I've been staying at Fido's. He's on vacay with his family so I've been able to just think. I've seen the posters in the neighborhood and I've been meaning to call but man, I'm just so whacked out right now.

I'm not ready to be a dad. I'm just a pup myself! How am I gonna raise six or seven little guys? I mean, I was the runt of my litter. I can't even take care of myself. Now I've gotta provide for the whole pack?

You know, one minute you're chasin' tail and the next you're supposed to be Ward Cleaver. I'm just not ready for this. I've never worked a day in my life!

Anyway, I guess I need to step up here. Be an alpha and do the right thing, you know? I'm not going to lie to you and say that things won't change. I'm going to be a family dog now and I'm not going to be able to hang like we used to.

So, I won't be coming back. (Sniff.) We had some great times. Some really great times. Man and, look, you did me a solid when you didn't get me fixed. You totally did me a solid. I'll never forget that. You had my back. And that time, you know, at the park when you met that blonde with that fine poodle . . . (sniff) . . . we tore up the town, man . . . we tore it up. It was our world but I guess we're all grown up, you know, and we have responsibilities now.

It's all good though. I'm ready for this. I can do this. And I'm gonna show everyone (sniff). My cousin Spot works on a farm up North and he's in good with the farmer there and I'm sure he can get me some work during the hunting season.

Maybe that's what I need, you know? To settle down, raise a family, earn an honest living. I mean, my old man walked out on me. I need to be there for these guys, right? Give them everything I didn't have until I met you.

All right, well, I'm gonna go. I just wanted to make sure we were cool. Much love to you.

Woof.

(497 WORDS)

DISCUSSION

Where does the letter writer sound like a dog, and where does he sound like a typical teenage guy? What's he trying to tell his owner, and what do you think the response would be? What might the female dog's point of view be? A cat's-eye view?

Diary Entries

"DEAR DIARY," BEGINS A FAMILIAR OPENING, "today I went skydiving for the first time." Or graduated from cosmetology school. Or decided to leave home with the family cat, Seymour. Maybe the skydiving ends on a broken leg or the cosmetology degree lands you a job at Harriet's Hair Haven or your husband sees you on the steps with the cat carrier and persuades you not to leave—which leads to another diary entry: from the hospital, at the hair salon, or in the basement with Seymour. But who are you writing for, and why?

Whether the diary is a red leatherette book with a golden clasp and key or a file kept on a flash drive, it's a record of what's happening. It can include just the bare facts—"I lured Seymour into the carrier with a pinch of catnip. I bought it at Pet World for $3.49"—or add emotions—"Home has become such a sad place, and only Seymour understands"—or analysis and strategy—"The problem was that Seymour wouldn't stop yowling. If I try again, it'll have to be without him."

Journals or diaries are like a series of letters written to oneself or an imaginary audience. What comes out depends on what experiences you've had that day. But if nothing eventful has happened, that doesn't mean the entry has to be dull. If you ate lunch alone in the break room today, the same cheese sandwich you've made for yourself since the start of September, you can riff on that. Consider how all American cheese slices taste as if they're cut from the same giant loaf, processed 500 feet underground in Wisconsin. Speculate on whether you might shift to cheddar. Will you ever meet a guy who hates cheese as much as your ex-boyfriend?

Bear in mind that, though people think of diaries as nonfiction, here they're being used as a vehicle for a piece of fiction, so there's no need to tell the truth. Ruminate. Explore. Be as judgmental as you like. The diary writer doesn't have to be you, of course. This urgent confider—or would someone lie in a diary?—can be the opposite of you: that person you're approaching on the park bench, his takeout coffee cup balanced on his laptop case, or someone you just imagine, a woman with half a dozen children, and she's pregnant again. She's recording how she feels and ends with what she thinks of her husband.

Traditionally, diary entries are for the writer, but if done well, they may prove intriguing for others. They can be as revealing as a peephole. They can emerge in whatever shape you like, from snapshots to lists to a running commentary on the daily routine. When the diary form becomes a conveyor for flash fiction, we read a first-person narration of what that person believes to be significant: a rock shaped like a heart, what the boss remarked about salaries, how much the writer detests her former best friend.

What makes for good diary entries? The interest depends on what you notice and how you register it. One inveterate journal keeper jotted down the price of everything he paid for, from groceries to appliances, for twenty-five years. Such is the nature of obsession, in which overemphasis and disproportion make for a strange new landscape. Here's a proposal for a diary entry as a piece of microfiction: the total cost of a day, itemized by emotion.

Journal entries can also have real gravity. The diary of Anne Frank is fraught with danger, encroaching Nazi forces that will eventually annihilate the diarist, along with millions of others. People know these facts about the Holocaust, but a diary puts a face on the tragedy.

Is there any incident one shouldn't write about? Try it. Make it brief but pungent. Diary writers don't worry about offending their audiences. You can always edit it later.

In flash fiction, you may have space for only a couple of entries at most (for fun, try ignoring this prescription and cram fifteen entries into two pages). But the passage of time is elastic: you can draw out the building of a sand sculpture at Point Pleasant beach so that every shovelful is accounted for, or you can dispense with it in a phrase. One particularly effective technique is to include past, present, and future in one recounting. Let's focus on the disastrous date with Peter (his car that smelled of wet dog, the bottle of cheap white wine he brought to the BYOB vegan restaurant), but also the preparations (half an hour in front of the mirror trying out eyeliner, mascara, and eye shadow) and the unpleasant aftermath (sour burps, and annoying texts from Peter for the next three days). Save a little space for reflection since a diary is, after all, a recording of impressions.

Who reads diaries, journals, or logs? Nowadays thousands of people may follow someone's blog, a shortened form of "web log," but it's the same idea. Though diary entries may be written in private, blog writers hope that multitudes will read them. In Oscar Wilde's play *The Importance of Being Earnest*, Cecily describes her diary to Algernon: "It is simply a very young girl's record of her own thoughts and impressions, and consequently meant for publication. When it appears in volume form I hope you will order a copy." If you learn anything from sculpting a diary entry into a short narrative, learn this: the reader is always a voyeur, looking through the keyhole that the author has provided.

Write whatever you like in your own diary, but if you're mocking up diary entries as a brief work of fiction, be brutally selective. Cut extraneous detail, rambling, repetition, abstractions . . . anything that doesn't directly contribute to the scene or mood you're trying to evoke. A good diary entry as a piece of fiction reveals something significant about an event and the person it happened to: I hate my roommate's boyfriend, Craig, and this afternoon I finally got the courage to tell him to stop crashing in our apartment. He gave me this look, as if I were some child who didn't understand about sex, and closed the door so gently, it was more annoying than if he'd slammed it. And he left his toothbrush, which he never even rinses.

Your account doesn't have to include everything that happened; in fact, it can't do that since the music of any day contains innumerable notes, which together form chords and harmony—or discord. You can even omit the part where you took Craig's toothbrush and did something to it that you now, um, kind of regret. Or you can make the act the focus of your whole entry. Whatever notes you choose, a successful diary entry pulls in readers and makes them want to read more. Who *is* this person recording these observations?

A word of caution: having your character come across a relative's diary from decades ago and read about a revealing incident is an over-used plot device. That doesn't mean you can't take this route, but if you do, you need to work hard to make it fresh. Maybe the diarist is a liar. Maybe a key page is missing—sorry, that's been done a lot, too.

An entry from a celebrity's diary is titillating because we want to know more about the lives of the rich and famous. Whom was she with the night that she left Channing Tatum's party early? Did the buffet really have the kind of caviar that costs $350 an ounce? What's it like talking to Scarlett Johansson when she's not acting? Does another actress there rely too much on prescription drugs to get through the evening?

EXERCISES

❶ Choose a celebrity whom you either know something about or are willing to research. Write a journal entry not about an over-the-top party but about the morning after, when the celebrity turns into just another person in an admittedly expensive bathrobe.

❷ A lot of writers like to mock up the diary of a madman or a person growing more and more insane. Instead, show a deranged person getting progressively saner.

READINGS

Will Stanton: "Barney"

August 30th. We are alone on the island now, Barney and I. It was something of a jolt to have to sack Tayloe after all these years, but I had no alternative. The petty vandalisms I could have forgiven, but when he tried to poison Barney out of simple malice, he was standing in the way of scientific progress. That I cannot condone.

I can only believe the attempt was made while under the influence of alcohol, it was so clumsy. The poison container was overturned and a trail of powder led to Barney's dish. Tayloe's defense was of the flimsiest. He denied it. Who else then?

September 2nd. I am taking a calmer view of the Tayloe affair. The monastic life here must have become too much for him. That, and the abandonment of his precious guinea pigs. He insisted to the last that they were better suited than Barney to my experiments. They were more his speed, I'm afraid. He was an earnest and willing worker, but something of a clod, poor fellow.

At last I have complete freedom to carry on my work without the mute reproaches of Tayloe. I can only ascribe his violent antagonism toward Barney to jealousy. And now that he has gone, how much happier Barney appears to be! I have given him complete run of the place, and what sport it is to observe how his newly awakened intellectual curiosity carries him about. After only two weeks of glutamic acid treatments, he has become interested in my library, dragging the books from the shelves, and going over them page by page. I am certain he knows there is some knowledge to be gained from them had he but the key.

September 8th. For the past two days I have had to keep Barney confined and how he hates it. I am afraid that when my experiments are completed I shall have to do away with Barney. Ridiculous as it may sound there is still the possibility that he might be able to communicate his intelligence to others of his kind. However small the chance may be, the risk is too great to ignore. Fortunately there is, in the basement, a vault built with the idea of keeping vermin out and it will serve well to keep Barney in.

September 9th. Apparently I have spoken too soon. This morning I let him out to frisk around a bit before commencing a new series of tests. After a quick survey of the room he returned to his cage, sprang up on the door handle, removed the key with his teeth, and before I could stop him, he was out the window. By the time I reached the yard I spied him on the coping of the well, and I arrived on the spot only in time to hear the key splash into the water below.

I own I am somewhat embarrassed. It is the only key. The door is locked. Some valuable papers are in separate compartments inside the vault. Fortunately, although the well is over forty feet deep, there are only a few feet of water in the bottom, so the retrieving of the key does not present an insurmountable obstacle. But I must admit Barney has won the first round.

September 10th. I have had a rather shaking experience, and once more in a minor clash with Barney I have come off second best. In this instance I will admit he played the hero's role and may even have saved my life.

In order to facilitate my descent into the well I knotted a length of three-quarter-inch rope at one-foot intervals to make a rude ladder. I reached the bottom easily enough, but after only a few minutes of groping for the key, my flashlight gave out and I returned to the surface. A few feet from the top I heard excited squeaks from Barney, and upon obtaining ground level I observed that the rope was almost completely severed. Apparently it had chafed against the edge of the masonry and the little fellow perceiving my plight had been doing his utmost to warn me.

I have now replaced that section of rope and arranged some old sacking beneath it to prevent a recurrence of the accident. I have replenished the batteries in my flashlight and am now prepared for the final descent. These few moments I have taken off to give myself a breathing spell and to bring my journal up to date. Perhaps I should fix myself a sandwich as I may be down there longer than seems likely at the moment.

September 11th. Poor Barney is dead an soon I shell be the same. He was a wonderful ratt and life without him is knot worth livving. If anybody reeds this please do not disturb anything on the island but leeve it like it is as a shryn to Barney, espechilly the old well. Do not look for my body as I will caste myself into the see. You mite bring a couple of young ratts an leeve them as a living memorial to Barney. Females—no males. I sprayned my wrist is why this is written so bad. This is my laste will. Do what I say an don't come back or disturb anything after you bring the young ratts like I said. Just females.

Goodby

(896 WORDS)

DISCUSSION

The naive diarist is a common device, an instance of dramatic irony: someone who doesn't know what's happening, though the reader does. At what point do you realize that the diarist in this story is seriously mistaken? Write an entry for Barney three years later.

Mark Budman: "The Diary of a Salaryman"

Today I was promoted to a junior coordinator of coordinating activities. This means I'll get a 3% salary raise spread over five years. This also means I get to stay at work longer.

Wife bore quintuplets. Was allowed to take three days off from work. Brought home the laptop and had a telecon during the delivery.

My cubicle mate was laid off. Had to pick up his workload. When I bent over the crib today, one of the quintuplets peed in my face, from a foot away. I think it was a boy.

Wife e-mailed me a picture of the kids on their first day in school.

Was promoted to an associate coordinator of coordinating activities. This means I'll get a 4% salary raise spread over five years. This also means I get to stay at work longer.

Today I saw a car with five teenagers leaving my garage. They waved at me. Is wife renting the garage out?

The new cubicle mate had a heart attack. While they were getting him on the stretcher, had a conversation with a guy from across the aisle. His name was Pete, and he's been with the company for twenty-four years. Twenty years in the same cubicle. Same as me.

Was promoted to a senior coordinator of coordinating activities. This means I'll get a 5% salary raise spread over five years. This also means I get to stay at work longer.

They laid me off today. Counted the remaining Valiums. Only three. Not enough for suicide.

Took my five grandchildren to a ball game today. Had ice cream in the park. My chest was heaving and a strange sound came from my throat. I guess they call it laughter.

Wife retired. Ran out of Viagra, but had sex with her anyway. She screamed and raked my back with her nails. Wow. The last time she'd done that was nine months before the quintuplets were born.

Got a call from work today. They want to re-hire me. E-mailed them a pic of myself flipping the bird.

Today is my last diary entry for a while. Too busy planting strawberries in my garden. Wife takes a bubble bath. Means it's going to be a busy night, too.

(372 WORDS)

DISCUSSION

What preoccupies the journal writer, and how do the incidents progress? What else would you like to know about him? How does time pass in the entries, and how would you chronicle it differently? What would the wife's entries look like?

Lists

TAKE A LOOK AT YOUR AVERAGE SHOPPING LIST: eggs, pretzels, apples, soda, bread, peanut butter, chicken, noodles, and frozen peas. What does it show about the consumer? Now take another shopping list, one that starts off with tofu and quinoa and moves on to granola and ginger root and dried lentils, and compare it to one that includes "5 lbs. chuck roast" and "hamburger meat." You are what you eat? But maybe the items aren't just for the person doing the buying. How would a shopping list indicate that the shopper has children? Or *is* a child? You can construct a profile from almost any list or at least make some educated guesses. If a list is detailed enough, you can even predict a plot: ammo, ski mask; fill gas tank. Consider not just items but also errands or a to-do list: pick up dry-cleaning, pick up kids from school, drop off kids at babysitter's house, meet Ryan at motel, pick up kids at 5:00, start dinner, pick up husband at station. Who's Ryan?

A list as flash fiction makes the point that any story has gaps, areas without information that readers have to fill in by themselves. A list piece simply takes that notion to an extreme, testing the reader's inferential powers. On the main character's to-do list are to buy a new amplifier, check [indecipherable] with ASCAP, and be at the recording studio Tuesday at 3:00. What does she do for a living? Add "replace ear-muffs" and "check snow blower." In what kind of climate does her family live? If the list includes a reference to placing an order with the ice man, when does the story take place? The list may also be annotated: for Fred; by 4 pm. It may have subsets or a hierarchy: Tues./Wed., or "mtg w/ Dan" underlined and placed after 1:00 and 2:30. You are what your days add up to.

A good flash fiction list piece has the appeal of those connect-the-dots pictures, which start out as a series of numbered points and end up, after you've penciled in all the connecting lines, as a sketch of a boy and a lion, a man playing golf, or a woman gazing at the moon. Another way to think of a short list fiction is through the painting technique of pointillism, in which a picture consists of myriad dots of paint, all of which together make a portrait when seen from a distance.

Consider the short list fiction as an index, a laundry list, bulleted items, or even a stream of consciousness: a woman's mind fixated on what she needs to bring on her trip to Sierra Leone. A list can show what someone is obsessed by: money, money, money. It can show what someone is trying not to think about: Kurt and his sexy smile but also the horrible meal he cooked for you last night. The list consists of recipes to send Kurt, all of which are meant to be seductive, especially those prosciutto love bites.

Consider the connections among the items: boots, mittens, parka, snowshoes. Slightly more difficult: lipstick, collar, perfume, laundry detergent. This last series should add up to something, though that total (adultery) may not be so obvious. In that way, a telling flash list fiction should also be greater than the sum of its parts.

EXERCISES

❶ Provide a list of items from a luxurious, old-fashioned bedroom: four-poster bed, mahogany night table, Indian throw rug, 1,000-thread-count Egyptian cotton sheets. Or check your wallet or purse, closet or dresser, and make a life from what you find there. Also try the refrigerator and the garage. What happens if one of those items goes missing? What would you like to add to the list? How does it differ from tomorrow's list?

❷ Build a list with one crucial item missing. What are the three essential items in your friend's life? How could you identify your father with five items? List seven items from long ago. Now do the same from 2070.

READINGS

Sei Shōnagon: "Annoying Things"
TRANSLATED BY IVAN MORRIS

One has sent someone a poem (or a reply to a poem) and, after the messenger has left, thinks of a couple of words that ought to be changed.

One has sewn something in a hurry. The task seems finished, but on pulling out the needle one discovers that one forgot to knot the end of the thread. It is also very annoying to find that one has sewn something back to front.

One day when the Empress was staying in the Southern Palace, she went to visit His Excellency, her father, in the western wing. I and the other ladies-in-waiting were gathered in the main building with nothing particular to do. We wandered along the corridors, trying to distract ourselves in one way or another. Then a messenger came from Her Majesty. "A robe is wanted in a hurry," we were told. "All of you are to get together and make sure that it is delivered to the Empress, fully sewn, before the next watch." We were then given some plain silk material.

My companions and I assembled at the front of the main hall, each of us taking a piece of silk and each determined to be the first to finish her work. We sat side by side, not facing each other, and started sewing at great speed. Nurse Myōbu, who did the wide sleeves, finished her work before anyone else. In her haste, however, she did not notice that she had sewn one piece of material inside out. Without even tying the final knot, she laid down the sleeves and stood up.

When it came to putting the different parts of the dress together at the back, we soon realized that there had been a mistake. The ladies laughed and scolded the nurse, saying, "You'd better do it over again properly." "And who do you suppose would admit she had made a mistake in sewing?" said the nurse. "With patterned silk, of course, one would have to start again if one had mistaken the front for the back, but with plain material like this what does it matter? If anyone has to do her work again, I don't see why it should be me. Ask the girls who still haven't finished their sewing."

Since she could not be persuaded, the rest of us had to start our work over again. It was really amusing to watch the expressions of Gen Shōnagon, Shin Chūnagon, and the others as they sat there plying their needles and muttering, "How does she think she can get away with it?" All this because Her Majesty intended to visit the Emperor that evening and had said, "I shall know that the one who gets her work done first really loves me."

It is annoying when a messenger delivers a letter to a person not meant to see it. If he simply admitted his mistake, it would not be so bad. But when he begins insisting that he merely carried out orders, it is really infuriating. If I were not afraid that someone might see me, I should rush up and strike him.

One has planted some nice clover or *susuki* grass and goes to have a look at it. What a painful and annoying experience to find someone with a long box and a spade who has carefully dug up the plants and is now carrying them away! If a gentleman were present, the fellow would not dare act like this. On being reproached, he answers, "I've only taken a little," and hurries off.

A retainer of some grand family comes to the house of a provincial official and speaks to him rudely with an expression implying, "You may find my manner annoying, but what can you do about it?"

A man snatches a letter that one does not want him to see and takes it into the garden, where he stands reading it. One runs after him in a rage. But one cannot go beyond the curtains; and there one stops, wishing that one could leap out at the man.

A woman is angry with her lover about some trifle and refuses to continue lying next to him. After fidgeting about in bed, she decides to get up. The man gently tries to draw her back, but she is still cross. "Very well then," he says, feeling that she has gone too far. "As you please." Full of resentment, he buries himself under his bedclothes and settles down for the night. It is a cold night and, since the woman is wearing only an unlined robe, she soon begins to feel uncomfortable. Everyone else in the house is asleep, and besides it would be most unseemly for her to get up alone and walk about. As the night wears on, she lies there on her side of the bed feeling very annoyed that the quarrel did not take place earlier in the evening when it would have been easy to leave. Then she begins to hear strange sounds in the back of the house and outside. Frightened, she gently moves over in bed towards her lover, tugging at the bedclothes, whereupon he annoys her further by pretending to be asleep. "Why not be stand-offish a little longer?" he asks her finally.

(879 WORDS)

DISCUSSION

Does Sei Shōnagon stray too much from one focus? Is she reasonable in her list of annoyances? What annoys you most in your daily life, and why? What would fix it, and can you create a work of flash fiction in which you do just that?

Steve Martin: "Disgruntled Former Lexicographer"

The following definition was discovered in the 1999 edition of the Random House dictionary. The crafting of this definition was the final assignment of Mr. Del Delhuey, who had been dismissed after thirty-two years with the company.

mutton (mut'n), *n.* [Middle English, from Old French *mouton, moton*, from Medieval Latin *multo, multon-*, of Celtic origin.] 1. The flesh of fully grown sheep. 2. A glove with four fingers. 3. Two discharged muons. 4. Seven English tons. 5. One who mutinies. 6. To wear a dog. 7. A fastening device on a mshirt or mblouse. 8. Fuzzy underwear for ladies. 9. A bacteria-resistant amoeba with an attractive do. 10. To throw a boomerang weakly. 11. Any kind of lump in the pants. (*Slang.*) 12. A hundred mittens. 13. An earthling who has been taken over by an alien. 14. The smallest whole particle in the universe, so small you can hardly see it. 15. A big nasty cut on the hand. 16. The rantings of a flibbertigibbet. 17. My wife never supported me. 18. It was as though I worked my whole life and it wasn't enough for her. 19. My children think I'm a nerd. 20. In architecture, a bad idea. 21. Define this, you nitwits. 22. To blubber one's finger over the lips while saying "bluh." 23. I would like to take a trip to the seaside, where no one knows me. 24. I would like to be walking along the beach when a beautiful woman passes by. 25. She would stop me and ask me what I did for a living. 26. I would tell her I am a lexicographer. 27. She would say, "Oh, you wild boy." Exactly that, not one word different. 28. Then she would ask me to define our relationship, which at that point would be one minute old. I would demur. But she would say, "Oh, please define this second for me right now." 29. I would look at her and say, "Mutton." 30. She would swoon. Because I would say it with a slight Spanish accent, at which I am very good. 31. I would take her hand, and she would notice me feeling her wedding ring. I would ask her whom she is married to. She would say, "A big cheese at Random House." 32. I would take her to my hotel room, and teach her the meaning of love. 33. I would use the American Heritage, out of spite, and read all the definitions. 34. Then I would read from the Random House some of my favorites among those that I worked on: "the" (just try it), "blue" (give it a shot, and don't use the word "nanometer"). 35. I would make love to her according to the O.E.D., sixth definition. 36. We would call room service and order tagliolini without looking it up. 37. I would return her to the beach, and we would say goodbye. 38. Gibberish in E-mail. 39. A reading lamp with a lousy fifteen-watt bulb, like they have in Europe.

Also: **a. muttonchops**: slicing sheep meat with the face. **b. muttsam**: sheep floating in the sea. **c. muttonheads**: the Random House people.

(529 WORDS)

DISCUSSION

At what point in the list do you realize that something's up? What can you trust in the list, and what can't you? Create your own list of definitions for a made-up word and, in the process, reveal something about the definer.

Fables

IMAGINE A FLASH FICTION in which the city isn't really a city; it's Freedom, a place where the doors are always open and people come and go as they please. The man who arrives from the countryside, where he worked in the fields: he's the History of Slavery. Why does someone tell a story in which the people and actions represent something far beyond their surface meaning? People tell fables to hold an audience while they teach. The fable of the six blind men and the elephant, in which each man sees a different part of the animal and claims it as the whole, is instructive. To the man who has hold of the tail, the elephant is like a snake. To the man who has hold of an ear, the elephant is like a fan. To the man feeling the elephant's side, the beast is like a wall. And so on. The lesson is that we each see only one part of reality. The story is brief, ending as soon as the message is relayed.

During the Middle Ages in Europe, when the Bible was the main book that people knew, most fables were Christian parables: for example, the prodigal son who returns to the family and is celebrated because the congregation rejoices when a sinner reforms. Yet over 1,000 years earlier, Aesop's fables about beasts taught proper conduct, to the point where we still use phrases from those brief stories: "Don't be a dog in the manger" means not to selfishly guard what you can't use.

The sentence comes from a fable about a little dog in a barn full of hay who yips and nips at the heels of the horses who come to eat the hay even though he himself can't use it. Eventually, the dog gets kicked. "Sour grapes" is a phrase uttered by someone who, unable to get what he wants, belittles that goal. In Aesop's fables, a fox who tries and tries to reach some grapes hanging from an arbor finally walks away, muttering that the grapes were probably sour anyway.

As you can see, these pieces emphasize simple character traits rather than complex psychology, a quick unfolding of events instead of a suspenseful tale. Any plot provided is a vivid pattern, bordering on myth. How can you tell your own fable? Start thinking in metaphors: in mathematical terms, how X = Y. What could a shopping trip in which you ended up buying nothing represent? Consider the saying "The journey, not the destination, matters"? How about a dinner where all the participants eat with their hands, even meat with gravy? Make up your own lesson here. What do you want to teach people? But don't be preachy, even if it's tempting at times. An implicit moral is okay, as long as it's not heavy-handed. Remember, your readers probably aren't children, and they can take a hint. Find ways to be both natural and symbolic at the same time. A rock is someone's hard heart. A butterfly is a free spirit. Only don't start lecturing. Or, as Duke Ellington said about his music: "You've got to find some way of saying it without saying it."

Be pithy. Try being amusing instead of earnest, or at least artfully diverting. That way, you get people's attention and slip them the lesson while they're focused on the story. A deeper issue is whether a parable must be moral. Whose morality? Whose code of ethics? Suppose you want to relate a short, short tale revealing that all people are slobs. See the previous paragraph's suggestion about the diners eating meat with gravy. Maybe the implied solution is forks and knives; maybe the suggestion is to avoid messy situations; maybe the point is that people (*sigh*) are people.

One additional observation: too many fables come across as flat or programmatic because they have their eye on the lesson at the end rather than on an emerging drama. Fables needn't have all the excitement of an action thriller but should at least have a high point, as well as characters worth watching. Consider the impact of action and surprises, too.

EXERCISES

❶ How would you illustrate that good things may come to those who wait—but those who wait too long get nothing?

❷ For a bit of fun, go against traditional wisdom:

You *can* buy happiness.

Beauty isn't just skin-deep: beautiful people really are better than others.

Crying over spilt milk gets results.

READINGS

Two monks, Tanzan and Ekido, were once traveling together down a muddy road. A heavy rain was still falling.

Coming around a bend, they met a lovely girl in a silk kimono and sash, unable to cross the intersection.

"Come on, girl," said Tanzan at once. Lifting her in his arms, he carried her over the mud.

Ekido did not speak again until that night when they reached a lodging temple. Then he could no longer restrain himself. "We monks don't go near females," he told Tanzan, "especially not young and lovely ones. It is dangerous. Why did you do that?"

"I left the girl there," said Tanzan. "Are you still carrying her?"

(113 WORDS)

DISCUSSION

What's the psychological drama going on between the two monks? Consider what kind of person derives satisfaction from reprimanding others. Rewrite the fable from the girl's point of view.

Raphael Dagold: "The Two Rats and the BB Gun"

Two rats were biding their time in an alley by a small pile of garbage, waiting for a boy with a BB gun to go in for dinner.

"Listen," one of the rats said to the other, "we'll be waiting here forever for that kid to go in. His mother's a drunk and is probably passed out on the couch. Let's make a run for it together. He'll be confused, and we know his aim is bad."

As the first rat made its dash, the second stayed behind to see how he fared. At that moment, the boy's mother called out:

"You come in here with that BB gun before I have to come out and get you."

Rolling his eyes, the boy didn't see the first rat cross to safety. The second, seeing his friend pass without a shot, walked confidently into the open. The boy, having stayed to spite his mother, took a last shot, his most careful of the evening.

Sometimes, chance intervenes where plans fail.

(169 WORDS)

DISCUSSION

What kind of intersections occur between the rats' realm and the world of people? Try rewriting this tale with an opposite message.

Anecdotes

AN APACHE CHIEF WAS INSTRUCTING HIS TRIBE to gather firewood for the upcoming winter, but he wanted to know how severe the season would be. So he called the National Weather Service and asked for a prediction. The man at the weather service said he'd check, then called back to tell the chief that it looked like a cold one. The chief had his people gather up more firewood then called the weatherman again, to make sure. The man said he'd get back to the chief, and when he did, he predicted a long, cold season. The chief ordered his people to strip the trees for even more fuel. Then he called the weatherman again, who this time forecast bitter cold for months.

This time, the chief was suspicious. "Every time I ask, the predictions grow worse. How do you know?"

"Well, the Apaches are collecting firewood like crazy," replied the weatherman.

Is this a story? Is it a joke? It's an anecdote, a usually humorous story that doesn't go on too long, which would risk losing the audience. The whole flash fiction is a lead-in to the payoff. Sometimes the piece can be extremely short:

"We are here on earth to help others. What on earth the others are here for, I don't know."

It can be a dialogue, usually between a straight man and a person who's funny, intentionally or not. Here's one attributed to the comedian Henny Youngman:

"How'd your first husband die?"

"Poison mushrooms."

"How'd your second husband die?"

"Poison mushrooms."

"And your third?"

"Fractured skull."

"What happened?"

"He wouldn't eat the poison mushrooms."

The world of anecdotes includes a lot of standard setups, ranging from the misunderstandings of children to three men in a bar. Or a priest, a rabbi, and a minister, or an American, an Englishman, and a Frenchman. This emphasis on threesomes is no coincidence. Many jokes, in fact most good stories, depend on a sturdy, three-legged structure: proposition, extension, and payoff. That is, the audience is given the situation; the situation is expanded; and in the final segment, the situation is stretched to absurdity. Another way to describe this structure is "repetition with a difference"; that is, an event happens, it happens again to show that it's a pattern, then it happens differently, or along comes something else that makes all the difference.

Good anecdotes may also illustrate the absurdity of our beliefs. Here's one supposedly about the Danish physicist Niels Bohr:

After Bohr won the Nobel Prize in 1922 for his work on atomic theory, the press came to interview him in his home, asking questions and taking pictures. As the last reporter was leaving, he spotted a horseshoe nailed above a doorframe, curved upward to catch luck. The reporter was astonished. "Surely, Dr. Bohr, you don't believe in such outmoded superstition as a horseshoe that brings luck!"

Dr. Bohr smiled. "Of course not. But I'm told that it will bring you luck whether you believe in it or not."

Bear in mind that an anecdote, like a fable, can evoke more than laughter. In fact, an anecdote is meant to be interesting or illustrative, and though humor often advances that point, it's not strictly necessary for an anecdote to work. The anecdote can show the absurdity of prejudice, how a clever plan can backfire, or how misunderstanding is just part of the human condition. Tell a good anecdote, and it'll stick in people's minds for a long time. Tell it well enough, and people will repeat it to others. It isn't necessarily funny; it's a good story. It provides clever imagery, a scene worth watching, some catchy dialogue, deft characterization, the unexpected, a fun reversal, a sudden realization—all aspects of storytelling but compressed into an anecdote.

One anecdote from someone's life—how she was supposed to pay someone to cut the grass, but saved money (and wrecked the lawn) by doing it herself—can reveal more than an entire chapter of her biography.

Because people who tell such stories don't want to bore their audiences, *timing, economy,* and *precision* are crucial.

Timing means how to pace yourself and where to place the emphasis in the story. If it's about your eight-year-old cousin April, pause a beat (or start a new paragraph) when you get to the part where she tried to lift her father because Mommy told her that poor Daddy needed a pick-me-up.

Economy means nothing extra and nothing wasted. Don't include April's brother Bill, even if he was part of what actually happened. Pare the story down to its essentials, which is good advice for any flash fiction.

Precision means getting the image just right. Describe how April reached out her arms like a forklift. Make sure you get April's innocent eight-year-old voice just right.

You can add ingenuity to that list since people delight in cleverness, even at the expense of others:

Two lawyers walked into a bar at lunch time, ordered drinks, opened their briefcases, and took out sandwiches. "Hey," said the bartender, "you can't eat food that you brought in here!" The two lawyers looked at each other, shrugged, and exchanged sandwiches.

This brief anecdote is about logic, language, and getting around limits. It also reveals a lot about how lawyers think—or how people think lawyers think.

Some pitfalls to beware of: don't merely adopt a breezy manner, with a lot of *emphasis* and exclamation points! If a situation is worth telling as an anecdote, just telling it well should be enough. An audience—your readers—will appreciate hearing it. Have fun. Make sure your readers do, too.

EXERCISES

❶ What's your favorite joke? Break it up into its parts, and expand it into a story, keeping the original proportions as much as possible.

❷ Start with a pun, such as "Weight for me!" or "We really knead the dough," and work your way backward, making up a way as to how the pun gets uttered.

READINGS

> A Russian peasant discovered a bottle in the field he was plowing, and when he opened it, a genie popped out. "I will grant three wishes," proclaimed the genie, "but whatever you ask for, your neighbor will get double." The peasant loathed his neighbor, who felt the same about him. For years, they'd cursed each other whenever they crossed paths. But the peasant didn't think hard enough about the consequences of the genie's proposition, because the first thing he asked for was ten thousand rubles. Instantly he was covered in rubles, enough to make a pool about him. He was ecstatic until he found out that his neighbor had just discovered twenty thousand rubles on his property. His joy vanished, he cursed his neighbor, and he tried to think about something more important than wealth. Finally, he smiled. "I'd like to marry the most beautiful woman in the world," he told the genie. At once, he held an absolutely gorgeous woman in his arms, who soon made him the happiest man around. Or so he thought. Somehow, at his neighbor's wed-

ding, held the next day, the bride was, unbelievably, twice as beautiful. It ruined all his pleasure to see his neighbor best him again. "I must do something about this," said the peasant to himself. Finally, he walked over to the genie, swallowed hard, and said, "Make me blind in one eye."

(232 WORDS)

DISCUSSION

What makes a person envious, and what can satisfy that envy? Does an opposite type exist with whom that person can get along? Consider some peculiar things to be envious about: a load of garbage, a physical handicap.

A woman won $25 million in the state lottery and told her husband, "Now get packing."

"That's great, honey!" he exclaimed. "But what should I pack? Hiking boots for a mountain vacation? A swimsuit for the beach?"

"I don't care. Just get packing."

(43 WORDS)

DISCUSSION

What does the anecdote imply about marriage and dependence? Would it be any different if the sexes were reversed? Consider how couples share misfortunes as well as good luck.

Prose Poems

TO CALL A PROSE POEM A POETIC DESCRIPTION or action sequence without much story is not to give credit for what it can do. It can beguile the reader with a mere paragraph. Of course, to discuss it at all, we should first define our terms. In this era, when free verse is the norm, i.e., when the majority of poems have neither rhyme nor consistent meter, what constitutes a poem?

Simply lines,
or the way
the words are arranged on
the page.

In fact, some writers in 19th-century Europe reacted against poetry in lines, though the term "prose poetry" was not yet in use. In his *Petits poèmes en prose*, published in 1869, Charles Baudelaire wrote fifty of them on subjects ranging from mirrors to money.

So what's a prose poem? With the last defining prop knocked out, poetry is not even a series of lines but instead a sequence of sentences. Neither plot nor character is necessary, though it may have both. Still, the focus of the piece is on pattern and imagery, displaying a fascination with language, toward some irreducible essence. One definition of poetry is concentrated prose. The prose poem may pursue an association (the link between navy blue and the blues) or a lyric moment (a pigeon flies overhead and drops a feather into your palm). Though it's not labeled prose poetry, the Book of Psalms in the King James Bible could easily qualify. Psalm 23, for instance, relies upon the metaphor of a person as a sheep and the deity as a shepherd: "Yea, though I walk through the valley of the shadow of death, I will fear no evil: for thou art with me; thy rod and thy staff they comfort me."

In the end, the strength or failing of this form is in its imagery: a baby carriage tumbling down the stairs, a man dressed all in red, dancing with his fingers. The sense of narrative or even the passage of time is unimportant; the point is lyric intensity, a burst of words that evokes a strong response from the reader. In the end, a prose poem may simply define a moment or a mood. As for how to end, go for an arresting image, preferably one with the accumulated weight of all the previous images: a toenail clipping—after all the other remnants of the dead woman have been gone through.

Consider using the equipment of most poets, figurative language. The doorknob is big as a grapefruit. The sky fits over the landscape as tightly as a helmet over a head. Acquaint yourself with poetic tropes, or figures of speech, from alliteration to zeugma. Assuming you know the basics like personification and simile, here are a few others:

anaphora	repeating the first word or phrase in successive clauses, as in "I didn't like coffee, I didn't like tea, and I didn't like the way he looked at me"
hypallage	a label applied to one term but really applying to another, as in "a crunchy bowl of cereal"
litotes	extreme understatement for effect, as in "He's no Einstein" to describe a dolt
metalepsis	using a figure of speech in a new context, as in "this spilt milk isn't worth dying over"
portmanteau	crunching two words to make a hybrid term, as in "those amusing definitions aren't real; they're just infotainment"

Finally: a good prose poem writer may work a lot with tonal qualities, even if the piece isn't meant to be read aloud. Think about alliteration, in which two words begin with the same sound, as in "same sound." Consider fast pace—"hippity-hoppity"—versus the opposite—"this slow pace." Of course, you can work on these qualities in your regular prose, as well.

EXERCISES

❶ Start with the color blue in your room, where it occurs and how. For each instance, devise a simile or metaphor for it: blue as a ———, a blue moon of a ———, and so on. After four or five instances, link the color to an episode in your life, and in describing it, color it all blue.

❷ Describe a specific, significant moment when you hurt someone deeply—but don't base it on a real incident. Too much poetry is assumed to be confessional. Make this one up. Use all five senses and at least five metaphors. Where do you end, and why?

READINGS

Yusef Komunyakaa: "Nude Interrogation"

Did you kill anyone over there? Angelica shifts her gaze from the Janis Joplin poster to the Jimi Hendrix, lifting the pale muslin blouse over her head. The blacklight deepens the blues when the needle drops into the first groove of "All Along the Watchtower." I don't want to look at the floor. *Did you kill anyone? Did you dig a hole, crawl inside, and wait for your target?* Her miniskirt drops into a rainbow at her feet. Sandalwood incense hangs a slow comet of perfume over the room. I shake my head. She unhooks her bra and flings it against a bookcase made of plywood and cinderblocks. *Did you use an M-16, a hand-grenade, a bayonet, or your own two strong hands, both thumbs pressed against that little bird in the throat?* She stands with her left thumb hooked into the elastic of her sky-blue panties. When she flicks off the blacklight, snowy hills rush up to the windows. *Did you kill anyone over there? Are you right-handed or left-handed? Did you drop your gun afterwards? Did you kneel beside the corpse and turn it over?* She's nude against the falling snow. *Yes.* The record spins like a bull's-eye on the far wall of Xanadu. *Yes, I* say. *I was scared of the silence. The night was too big. And afterwards, I couldn't stop looking up at the sky.*

(230 WORDS)

DISCUSSION

How do sex and death commingle in this piece, and to what effect? How does the other imagery contribute? Where's the climax? Suppose the person's answers to the repeated question were no.

Len Kuntz: "Story Problems"

She says I have problems, issues with words. She says if she didn't know better she'd think my teeth were Scrabble chips and that I eat Banana-gram for breakfast. She long ago tossed my laptop into a bath of steaming water. Now she hides pens. Each morning there's a bonfire to rid our place of paper. In olden days, young rabbis would memorize the entire Old Testament, word for word. In that way they not only proved their dedication and prowess, but they ensured the story would endure.

(88 WORDS)

DISCUSSION

Why are writers such a pain in the neck at times? Why do they feel that preserving their words is so important? Substitute another obsession here.

Soliloquies, Rants, Riffs, and Themes

WHO'S THAT GUY ON THE STREET CORNER, shouting about the end of the world? Maybe he grows tiresome after a while, but you won't hear him that long. This is flash fiction, after all. In fact, one intense voice declaiming can have a real pull. Playwrights know this lesson: think of Hamlet's famous "To be or not to be" soliloquy, or Macbeth's "Tomorrow and tomorrow and tomorrow" speech after the death of his wife. They have a real message, and they deliver it well.

The rant gets its force from content and style. What's the speech about, and is it focused or all over the place? It's about never getting a break in life, with a growl for emphasis. It includes the time you were fired for standing up to the boss, as well as the time you were canned for missing too many days of work. Bear in mind that behind a scattered performance is often an underlying theme. What provoked the outburst? Receiving a lousy job-performance rating for the third month in a row? If it's a monologue, is it to oneself or to an imaginary audience? To your best friend, who's heard it all before? Does it conclude anything? "Nobody loves me enough"? Any accompanying action?—don't just stamp a foot or smite your brow.

How long does a rant go on before it gets to be a drag? What can rescue it from that danger? Imagery. Maybe you know a guy who complains wonderfully, wittily, so you let him go on and on because he's entertaining. Last week, he complained that his coworker in sales was a six-sided idiot and proceeded to describe all six sides. You also know a teenage girl who just whines, and that's no fun at all. The subject may also be unrewarding or trivial. Maybe if she had a plan to help world hunger, rather than going on and on about her dislike of pancakes from Corso's Café, someone would listen. Or if she could devastatingly sum up her last experience at the café. Or what if the rant is just extremely offensive? Always consider your audience.

Since another term for this flash fiction is "dramatic monologue," remember to dramatize. Forceful language can help, not just the usual nouns and verbs. For "had," substitute "possessed"; replace "dog" with "my pet monster." Also, to think only of highly articulate speeches or polysyllables is a mistake. Sometimes the most wretched, awkward language reaches out and grabs the audience by the scruff of the neck.

As for a riff, the term is borrowed from jazz: a short musical phrase repeated throughout the work, even as the harmony or chords change. In writing, a riff is a recurrent phrase in a piece that may acquire different levels of meaning, depending on the context. It can hold the piece together thematically; it can provide rhythm and counterpoint. Take the phrase "meant no harm": first the character of the mother says that she meant no harm in letting her son's friend stay the night, then she adds that she meant no harm in letting the friend climb the ladder to the attic, then she notes that she meant no harm in icing down the kid's leg after he fell, rather than see whether anything was broken, then— but you get the idea.

A theme may also hold together a piece: a meditation on cats or a focus on all the bad parties you've attended recently. Feel free to em- broider on your experience since the work is supposed to be fiction. One cat was three feet tall and would come scampering whenever you whistled "Three Blind Mice." Angelica's Fish Grotto serves the worst shrimp cocktail in Indiana.

Have fun. It's your chance to rant.

EXERCISES

❶ What exercises you? That is, what gets you in high dudgeon? What pisses you off? Be specific: not just "I hate snow," but a recall of the last five times you had to shovel the driveway, the way your car skidded on the access road to the turnpike, the brown-gray stuff that the snow turned into the third day, and so on.

❷ Now invert the previous exercise: how would someone rant against you? If you can't bear this idea, you can also get some mileage out of what you love (think of a rave review for a restaurant, but don't be sappy, and do provide details).

Note: because these are fiction exercises, the topics don't have to really represent you. They can show the viewpoints of someone you know or of a character you just made up.

READINGS

Christine Byl: "Hey, Jess McCafferty"

Hey, Jess McCafferty, what are you doing here? I've never seen you in the store before. I bet you're looking for my sister, but she isn't here, and even if she was, I'd say, "Louisa isn't here right now," because she doesn't love you anyway, Jess. I know you know who I am, but you walk by without saying anything—what's so interesting about the floor? Do you know I'm by myself? Dad trusts me to keep track of things, even though I'm two years younger than Louisa, and besides, she has better things to do than hang around in a hardware store. She says, "You'll un-derstand when you're sixteen, Callie." But I like the smell of the linseed oil Dad rubs into the countertop, and the light in the glass above the front door. I can read when the store's empty. Louisa, she likes things faster than I do. "You can sleep when you're dead," she says.

You think my sister's in love with you, don't you, Jess? I know she's made you think so, sneaking out the window at night, dropping onto the flowers, into your hands. But see, sisters get things about each other, and that's how I know, she's making a fool out of you, Jess. She likes you okay, the way your eyes make her feel, like there's something hot under-neath her skin. But like and love are two different things, Jess. "Louisa, you better watch out," I tell her, but she already knows.

You only smile at me because I'm her little sister, otherwise you'd never even see a girl like me, would you? Well, you know what, Jess, Louisa thinks I'm beautiful. She lets me borrow her clothes—I'm wearing her jeans right now, the ones she embroidered at the hem. We wear the same size, but she likes them tight and I like them baggy. "You're so lucky, Callie, you're so skinny," my sister says, and she won't eat at din-ner sometimes and she stands in front of the mirror at night and sucks in her cheeks and holds the skin around her middle with both hands. Hey, Jess, did you know that Louisa and I have shared a room since I was born? I could tell my sister from a hundred strangers lying down in the dark just by the way she breathes.

I know how far she lets you go, Jess. Does that shock you? She tells me stuff she doesn't even tell her friends. Never mind what she tells you. I heard her say, "Oh Dad, don't worry, he's definitely *not* my boy-friend." She rolls her eyes and twists her necklaces around her hand so they pinch the skin on her neck. If I told you that right now, Jess, you'd drop your eyes and smile and you'd act like you didn't care, but if my sister didn't love you and you knew it, you'd care.

Anyway, Louisa is smarter than you think. Sometimes she lies on the bed on her back and she traces the outline of herself. She presses her finger into the top of her head, runs it along her hair, down over her ear, under her chin where it meets her neck and all the way down until she can't reach without bending and then she starts up the other side. Let me tell you, Jess, Louisa knows where she starts and where she ends.

What are you up to, Jess, running those hands over everything? Don't you know what you're looking for? I bet it's not a socket set. I'm not going to ask you if you need any help. If you need it, you can ask. Do you even know my name? I think you do, even though I know Louisa doesn't talk about me when you guys park in your junky pickup, or lie out in the back field with your hands up her shirt. I've watched you, Jess, the way you jog alongside her in the dark as she tilts her head away. In the morning, I can see the places where your feet pressed down in the wet grass, and she tells me where you went and what you did anyway, so you've got no secrets from me, Jess McCafferty.

Are you still watching to see if she's going to come out from the curtain behind the register? Are you looking at me? You think I don't see you because I'm reading, but if you were close, you'd see it's just a catalog for lawn tools. You're used to the feel of eyes on you, anyway, aren't you, Jess, all the girls in three grades crazy about you, something about your tan arms and faded shirts and the way your bones fit under the skin of your face.

But come on, Jess, you can see she isn't here so you might as well leave because you are starting to look aimless, and I don't think that's how you want to look. My dad will be back any minute, and he'll say something to you, you can bet on it. Is this how you first looked at Louisa, quick meeting her eyes, then smiling after you looked away? You can't love her like she needs to be loved, Jess McCafferty. She's too much for you, and deep down, you already know it. You need a simpler kind of girl, and I'm not saying she's me, but just think twice about Louisa.

Hey, Jess McCafferty, you think I can't see you over there? I saw you slip that in your pocket, looking at me between the shelves. Who do you think you are? It doesn't matter what I say, does it, Jess. I can't change how you feel about Louisa. But I could get you in such trouble. I could tell my father just like that, you know. I'd do it, too, watch me. Hey Dad, I'd say, Jess McCafferty was around here today, looking for Louisa, taking what isn't his.

(999 WORDS)

DISCUSSION

Does the speaker's rant end the same place it starts? How would it change if the sexes were reversed? What might the father's rant or Jess's rant be like?

John Edgar Wideman: "Witness"

Sitting here six floors up on my little balcony when I heard shots and saw them boys running. My eyes went straight to the lot beside Mason's bar, and I saw something black not moving in the weeds and knew a body was lying there and knew it was dead. A 15-year-old boy, the papers said. Whole bunch of sirens and cops and spinning lights the night I'm talking about. I watched till after they rolled him away and then everything got quiet again as it ever gets round here, so I'm sure the boy's people not out there that night. Didn't see them till next morning. I'm looking down at those weeds. A couple's coming slow on Frankstown with a girl by the hand, had to be the boy's baby sister. They pass terrible Mason's and stop exactly next to the spot the boy died. How did they know. Then they commence to swaying, bowing, hugging, waving their arms about. Forgive me, Jesus, but look like they grief dancing, like the sidewalk too cold or too hot they had to jump around not to burn up. How'd his people find the spot. Could they hear my old mind working to guide them, lead them like I would if I could get up out this damn wheelchair and take them by the hand.

(224 WORDS)

DISCUSSION

How might this story be different if the victim weren't black? Why doesn't the wheelchair-bound narrator speak up? What exactly is it that preoccupies him? What's the neighborhood like?

Perfect Miniatures

FLASH FICTION DEMANDS that the writer accomplish a great deal in a small space, but what kind of complete narrative can you actually pull off in just a few pages? We've already talked about short pieces that detail only one incident, those that sketch a character, some that are based on letters, and so on. How about if you're wedded to traditional plot and character and don't want to give that up? In that case, you should try working on miniatures. The term *miniatures* in this usage refers to those tiny pictures you occasionally see in art museums: a full portrait of someone, but only 3″ × 3″. The body is tiny, but with everything in perfect proportion. How did the artist execute such a picture? Did he use a tiny brush?

Once again, representation is key. That's what art equals, anyway, not the thing itself—a dog, a house, an unhappy marriage—but what you see on the canvas or the page: a mournful-looking basset hound, an A-frame cabin, two people in the same bed, sleeping as far apart from each other as they can.

Miniatures intensify the principles of representation. In a story, if you represent a thing by a type, you're taking some large idea or shape, such as justice, and portraying it representationally, such as through a series of court cases. In a miniature, you don't have the time or space for that kind of development. You've got to move, and fast. You want justice? Give us a court verdict. Trying to portray a friendly town but don't have time for the ice cream truck, the kind-hearted policeman, and the pedestrians who smile and say hello? Give us just a crossing guard helping a kid across the street.

In poetry, this kind of compression may be metonymy, synecdoche's cousin, which uses a related part to represent the whole, as in the familiar saying, "The pen is mightier than the sword," where the pen is obviously "writing," and the sword is a stand-in for warfare—or peaceable means of persuasion as opposed to violence.

You can see how this kind of imagery works: by suggestion rather than full description, by having the reader eke out a phrase or a line into a whole paragraph or page, based on the reader's experience. The question is how one pares down to the essential details.

Let's take a man's body. We could sum him up, from his male-pattern baldness and bullet-shaped head to his beer belly and hammer toes. But instead, think about what you're trying to convey specifically, and leave out all the rest. If he's old-fashioned, give him one of those curving mustaches that you can see in photographs from the Victorian era. Or a cut of clothing that no one wears anymore. If the point is that he's muscular, just give us a shot of his pecs.

The same simplification applies to plot. The guy's unlucky in love not three times, but just once, with the other times hinted at in a sentence to make your point that he's a loser. The sameness of a routine that you'd ordinarily spend a page on, to demonstrate the rote movements, you can outline with a detail and note that it repeats daily. Practice learning how to select what's crucial and omit the rest.

In a sense, a perfect miniature is like those capsule book reviews in 100 words or fewer. Instead of containing an introduction to the author, a framing of the subject, a plot summary, an analysis of the author's technique, and so on, these mini-reviews cut right to the chase (insert better metaphor here). The opening is both a lead-in and the beginning of the plot outline; the next sentence introduces the characters; the third tells us what's at stake and how the book progresses; the fourth comments on the author's skill; and the fifth pronounces judgment. If pressed, you could probably omit sentences four and five, smuggling in a bit of each into sentences one through three. What's omitted, and why? Note that leaving out certain details heightens others.

EXERCISES

❶ Below is a five-sentence character. Cut out what you think can be deleted without too much damage to the description. Rewrite it so that it's both tight and evocative.

Charles Henry was a large man, upward of 275 pounds, who made the rickety staircase where he roomed tremble every time he came down from the third floor. He ate prodigiously, over 5,000 calories a day, from eggs and toast and bacon and more eggs and bacon every morning to his late-evening snack of pretzel sticks and cheese dip. But he kept his weight from ballooning to alarming levels by dint of nightly exercise: dressed in a pair of old long johns, pulling on an old rowing machine in the basement, next to the furnace, which seemed to roar encouragingly after every stroke. By day, Charles worked in Denton's, the last surviving furniture store in Greenville, selling sofas and armchairs, tables and cabinets, from nine in the morning to six in the evening. He had a sometime-girlfriend named Maxine, who worked across the square in the First National Bank but who liked to drop in on Charles during her lunch hour and lounge in one of Denton's top-of-the-line sofas with her feet up.

❷ Now do the same with this plot:

While he was helping a couple pick out a bed, Charles heard a noise from the front of the store, as if something was scraping along the floor. He turned his head to see a scrawny man desperately trying to lug a table out the door. No one else was in the store just then—Ted was on his lunch break—so Charles simply shouted, "You put that back right now, you hear?" But that just had the effect of making the man haul all the harder, till suddenly he had it out the entrance. Charles lumbered after him like a bull in a button-down shirt, but the guy had already let go of the table and was halfway down the street, looking back at Charles and headed right for an oncoming truck.

READINGS

John Collier: "The Chaser"

Alan Austen, as nervous as a kitten, went up certain dark and creaky stairs in the neighborhood of Pell Street, and peered about for a long time on the dim landing before he found the name he wanted written obscurely on one of the doors.

He pushed open this door, as he had been told to do, and found himself in a tiny room, which contained no furniture but a plain kitchen table, a rocking chair, and an ordinary chair. On one of the dirty buff-colored walls were a couple of shelves, containing in all perhaps a dozen bottles and jars.

An old man sat in the rocking-chair, reading a newspaper. Alan, without a word, handed him the card he had been given. "Sit down, Mr. Austen," said the old man very politely. "I am glad to make your acquaintance."

"Is it true," asked Alan, "that you have a certain mixture that has—er—quite extraordinary effects?"

"My dear sir," replied the old man, "my stock in trade is not very large—I don't deal in laxatives and teething mixtures—but such as it is, it is varied. I think nothing I sell has effects which could be precisely described as ordinary."

"Well, the fact is—" began Alan.

"Here, for example," interrupted the old man, reaching for a bottle from the shelf. "Here is a liquid as colorless as water, almost tasteless, quite imperceptible in coffee, milk, wine, or any other beverage. It is also quite imperceptible to any known method of autopsy."

"Do you mean it is a poison?" cried Alan, very much horrified.

"Call it cleaning fluid if you like," said the old man indifferently. "Lives need cleaning. Call it a spot-remover. 'Out, damned spot!' Eh? 'Out, brief candle!'"

"I want nothing of that sort," said Alan.

"Probably it is just as well," said the old man. "Do you know the price of this? For one teaspoonful, which is sufficient, I ask five thousand dollars. Never less. Not a penny less."

"I hope all your mixtures are not as expensive," said Alan apprehensively.

"Oh, dear, no," said the old man. "It would be no good charging that sort of price for a love-potion, for example. Young people who need a love-potion very seldom have five thousand dollars. Otherwise they would not need a love-potion."

"I am glad to hear you say so," said Alan.

"I look at it like this," said the old man. "Please a customer with one article, and he will come back when he needs another. Even if it *is* more costly. He will save up for it, if necessary."

"So," said Alan, "you really do sell love-potions?"

"If I did not sell love-potions," said the old man, reaching for another bottle, "I should not have mentioned the other matter to you. It is only when one is in a position to oblige that one can afford to be so confidential."

"And these potions," said Alan. "They are not just—just—er—"

"Oh, no," said the old man. "Their effects are permanent, and extend far beyond the mere casual impulse. But they include it. Oh, yes they include it. Bountifully. Insistently. Everlastingly."

"Dear me!" said Alan, attempting a look of scientific detachment. "How very interesting!"

"But consider the spiritual side," said the old man.

"I do, indeed," said Alan.

"For indifference," said the old man, "they substitute devotion. For scorn, adoration. Give one tiny measure of this to the young lady—its flavor is imperceptible in orange juice, soup, or cocktails—and however gay and giddy she is, she will change altogether. She will want nothing but solitude and you."

"I can hardly believe it," said Alan. "She is so fond of parties."

"She will not like them any more," said the old man. "She'll be afraid of the pretty girls you may meet."

"She'll actually be jealous?" cried Alan in a rapture. "Of me?"

"Yes, she will want to be everything to you."

"She is, already. Only she doesn't care about it."

"She will, when she has taken this. She will care intensely. You'll be her sole interest in life."

"Wonderful!"

"She'll want to know all you do," said the old man. "All that has happened to you during the day. Every word of it. She'll want to know what you are thinking about, why you smile suddenly, why you are looking sad."

"That is love!" cried Alan.

"Yes," said the old man. "How carefully she'll look after you! She'll never allow you to be tired, to sit in a draft, to neglect your food. If you are an hour late, she'll be terrified. She'll think you are killed, or that some siren has caught you."

"I can hardly imagine Diana like that!" cried Alan, overwhelmed with joy.

"You will not have to use your imagination," said the old man. "And, by the way, since there are always sirens, if by any chance you *should*, later on, slip a little, you need not worry. She will forgive you, in the end. She'll be terribly hurt, of course, but she'll forgive you—in the end."

"That will not happen," said Alan fervently.

"Of course not," said the old man. "But if it does, you need not worry. She'll never divorce you. Oh, no! And, of course, she herself will never give you the least, the very least, grounds for—not divorce, of course— but even uneasiness."

"And how much," said Alan, "how much is this wonderful mixture?"

"It is not as dear," said the old man, "as the spot-remover, as I think we agreed to call it. No. That is five thousand dollars; never a penny less. One has to be older than you are to indulge in that sort of thing. One has to save up for it."

"But the love-potion?" said Alan.

"Oh, that," said the old man, opening the drawer in the kitchen table and taking out a tiny, rather dirty-looking phial. "That is just a dollar."

"I can't tell you how grateful I am," said Alan, watching him fill it.

"I like to oblige," said the old man. "Then customers come back, later in life, when they are rather better-off, and want more expensive things. Here you are. You will find it very effective."

"Thank you again," said Alan. "Good-bye."

"*Au revoir*," said the old man.

(1,057 WORDS)

DISCUSSION

As psychologists have noted, love is a power relationship. Change this power imbalance and create a different flash fiction. Or have the old man offer something else.

Jeffrey Whitmore: "Bedtime Story"

"Careful, honey, it's loaded," he said, re-entering the bedroom.

Her back rested against the headboard. "This for your wife?"

"No. Too chancy. I'm hiring a professional."

"How about using me?"

He smirked. "Cute. But who'd be dumb enough to hire a lady hit man?"

She wet her lips, sighting along the barrel.

"Your wife."

(54 WORDS)

DISCUSSION

How does distrust create its own plot? Apply the lesson of this story, in a nonfatal way, to the beginning of a relationship.

Intermission:
Cutting Down

TIME TO FOCUS ON THE ART OF REDUCTION. You've finished your story, which weighs in at 526 words, 26 too many for the M. M. Memorial Flash Fiction Contest. Or maybe your flash fiction about an archery match seems perfect—until your friend and best reader tells you that all those *thwocks* grow monotonous. Maybe you've done what so many authors in command of powerful effects do: registered the slap and the reaction but then described them, as well. No need to show him blush *and* say he's really embarrassed. Or you just use too many words in too many phrases in various paragraphs composed of too many sentences like this.

No author wants to be accused of padding, but a flash fiction writer really has to make every word count, especially when there's a word count. Consider TMI, Too Much Information, as it applies to how your character gets ready for work. Claiming you included some of that "for the rhythm" isn't a good excuse.

Go ahead, start paring down—but how? You can approach the task in several ways:

▸ Slashing, in which a whole paragraph may go if it's just unnecessary background. Who really needs to know that Roy wears a hairpiece, that he puts it on a stand when he goes to bed, that it's his third in three years . . . though these seemed like fun facts at the time you wrote them. In a story that may be no more than a page, that may translate into cutting a sentence here and another there. No need even to let us know that Roy is balding, unless the plot hinges on it.

▸ Microsurgery, in which you cut individual words.

Delete "the fact." "He couldn't stand the fact that she smoked" becomes "He couldn't stand that she smoked" or, even better, "He couldn't stand her smoking."

Cut expletives. No, not swear words; rather, weak constructions like "it is" and "there are," which begin far too many sentences. Who needs "There was a cat on the table" when "A cat was on the table" serves the purpose better, and "A large cat covered the table" replaces the weak "to be" verb with something more active? Cutting out the expletive in your sentence means that you get directly to the subject and may even force you to rephrase more actively: "It was not a happy time for her" becomes "She hadn't been happy all of April."

Cut dialogue tags. Do you really need that ping-pong game of "he said, she said"? How many replacement verbs have you cooked up for "said"? "Fumed," "sighed," "stated," "pronounced," "averred" . . . Cut "he said" and, in its place, put a short action-verb sentence. That will identify the speaker and build some action. Not

"I don't like you," she said.

but

"I don't like you." She yawned.

That way, you can cut the next two sentences, which were all about how boring she found him.

Cut "very." Not "very bright," but "brilliant." Not "very hungry," but "starving."

Cut adjectives and adverbs whenever possible. Not "brilliant woman," but "genius." Not "yelled angrily," but simply "yelled."

Cut creeping A&B-ism. "I am sick and tired of your constant and never-ending fits and tantrums." Nah. "I'm tired of your tantrums."

Note that cutting away usually strengthens a line of prose rather than weakening it because the emphasis doesn't have to be shared among so many words: the difference between "Go to your room" and "Go!"

Some writers have even developed an entire aesthetic philosophy of cutting. Below are the first two rules from "Imagisme," published in a 1913 issue of the magazine *Poetry*, supposedly by a writer named F. S. Flint, but really cooked up by Ezra Pound and a couple of friends.

1. Direct treatment of the "thing," whether subjective or objective.
2. To use absolutely no word that does not contribute to the presentation.

Pound intended these rules to apply to poetry, but they apply just as well to flash fiction, where a concentrated essence is crucial. Cut the abstractions, such as your two lines about unfair due process, and give us instead a phrase to evoke that concept, a crooked lawyer. Instead of truth, justice, and the American way, give us Superman. William Carlos Williams, a contemporary of Pound's, put it this way in his poem *Paterson*: "no ideas but in things."

Get rid of words that are there for padding or rhythm or just for the hell of it. If a word doesn't help the story along in plot or characterization or imagery, lose it. Be brutal. Sometimes the loveliest cluster of words you've got doesn't help in advancing the narrative. Hemingway famously said to find the one sentence in the story you're most proud of, and cut it, on the assumption that it's too showy.

Some additional tips:

Read your work out loud to hear where it can be condensed. You can often catch errors that way, too.

What you might consider a space constraint might also spur resourcefulness. Necessity is the mother of all sorts of ingenuity.

When deciding what to cut and what to save, decide what your story's about, then proceed along that theme. If your piece is about the indignity of growing old, you can omit that scene when your character was nineteen or reduce it to a one-sentence memory.

Cutting isn't just your problem. All writers face this issue. Here's a 497-word story about it:

Bruce Taylor: "Exercise"

Take a story from real life, one you are having trouble focusing. Cut the story in half. Cut it in half again. What you're left with is the essentials of the story you will be able to see more clearly.
(257 words)

They have said nothing to each other for weeks except what matters to the day, the children, the budget or the dog. He is upstairs at his office window. She is reading in a chaise longue in the shade some book her recently widowed mother gave her. She sighs, he imagines, at how it was an easy mistake for a young girl to make, a less likely error, perhaps, for a man so much older.

Who remembers mostly a white dress, a waist your hands could fit around, the scent of Juicy-Fruit and Noxzema. When he asks what's wrong, she always says she's happy; the only thing is, if he were sometimes a little happier a little more often too . . .

What she thinks of him now he doesn't even know, but fears it's so much less than what she thought at first, when he was what he can't imagine now, and obviously isn't to her now, and why and why? In the grief of his fifties, hard liquor sits him down to pray.

They treat each other as tenderly at least as they'd treat a relative or friend, a needy stranger or the obligatory guest. Whatever it is they might be discussing escapes to the underside of the birch leaves in the gathering breeze. The lights across the river are brighter and seem more distant than the stars. The swallows give way to the bats and a tiny spider spins at the ruined screen a web someone less desperate might be tempted to take as a metaphor.
(128 words)

They have said nothing to each other for weeks except what matters to the day, the children, the budget or the dog. He is upstairs at his office window. She sighs, he imagines, at where love has led her and how it was an easy mistake for a young girl to make.

He remembers a white dress, a waist your hands could fit around, the scent of Juicy Fruit and Noxzema—he wants to ask her what she remembers.

They treat each other as tenderly at least as they'd treat a relative or friend, a needy stranger or the obligatory guest. Whatever it is they might be discussing escapes to the underside of the birch leaves. The lights across the river are brighter and seem more distant than the stars.

(63 words)

They have said nothing to each other for weeks except what matters to the day. She sighs at where love has led her. He remembers a white dress. They treat each other as they'd treat a stranger. Whatever they might be discussing escapes to the underside of the birch leaves. The lights across the river are brighter and more distant than the stars.

DISCUSSION

What details stick out most to you? Which version do you like best, and why?

EXERCISES

❶ Take any story you've written that's longer than five pages and try to make it into a piece of flash fiction, which we'll call 1,000 words or fewer. Note: you have to first decide what your story's really about so you can cut away the other material.

❷ Take someone else's story, and perform the same kind of cutting job. What decisions did you make and why? Was is it easier than working with your own material or harder?

Surrealism

SINCE FORM OFTEN DICTATES STYLE, some people think that flash fiction shouldn't follow a typical narrative flow. Why strive for real characterization and a climax in a few pages? Instead, consider the sheer brevity of what you're attempting and go for quick, oddball effects. A guy goes for a walk in the park and meets an alligator named Sam. The two of them stop by a hot dog stand and order a couple with the works. A woman skateboards by and steals their lunch. In the nearby sycamore, two squirrels laugh over the incident.

Not your average linear sequence. And check your skepticism at the door. This is the language of dreams, sometimes embodied in prose poems. It's the art of the collage and the surreal jump cut, where disjointed images (alligator in the park, theft by skateboard, squirrel talk) merge to make you think about the fragmented nature of reality. It exploits the incidental bordering on the irrational, often through unexpected juxtapositions. But that's one definition of originality: two common objects—or traits or events—spliced at an odd angle. It partakes of surrealism, which involves an odd juxtaposition of events and characters, intersecting planes of reality as in a dreamscape. At its extreme, it is "beautiful as the chance meeting on a dissecting table of a sewing machine and an umbrella," in the words of the surrealist writer Isidore Ducasse.

With this technique in mind, set up a drive to the bank, but not for the usual plot device of a hold-up. This time, give us a woman carrying a parakeet in a cage that she wishes to put in her safe-deposit box. Maybe the bank manager starts chatting with the bird in Greek. Meanwhile, the chandelier overhanging the main room of the bank takes on a different shape every time someone stares at it. These disparate actions and images, when juxtaposed, take on the aspect of a collage where cut-out shapes commingle on the page.

Donald Barthelme, a consummate postmodern ironist, called collage *the* art form of the twentieth century. Sometimes life seems to proceed in just such a fashion. Consider the work of Richard Brautigan, who begins a two-pager called "Sand Castles" this way: "Strange fences grow on Point Reyes Peninsula which is fastened like a haunted fingerprint to the California coast. Odd perspectives are constantly drifting out of sight or becoming too intimate in this place where white medieval Portuguese dairies suddenly appear cradled by cypress trees and then disappear as if they had never really been there at all." The speaker's trip to Point Reyes consists largely in what he observes and how he puts it. If you want to enliven your own journey in a brief space, the stuff of every day must become somewhat off-kilter. Caught in a traffic jam? A car barks at a bus. Overhead, the traffic light turns purple.

New connections are there, waiting to be drawn by either you or your readers. They should be thought-provoking. The movement in such a flash fiction comes from the roving eye—or restless mind. Your piece could just as easily be a brief stream of consciousness. The flash fictions in Robert Olen Butler's collection *Severance* are nothing but that: the thoughts of people who've just been decapitated and have about a minute and a half of life remaining. These unfortunates range from John the Baptist to a Texan truck driver: no more sensory input, just memories and associations. Here's Medusa, who has a habit of turning men to stone, till Perseus cuts off her head: "I love my living hair these serpents whisper when men come close each strand with a split tongue hissing my desire for them I shake my dear children my tresses down and they curl back up their black eyes flashing and the man cries out at my beauty . . ." If you don't find this passage petrifying, you haven't read hard enough.

Do you need closure in these metaphor-spliced shorts? No, but try to end on some haunting image, like a cigarette butt, long abandoned, that suddenly bursts into flame.

EXERCISES

❶ Link these five images in a sketch of 500 words:

> a tropical sunset
> a half-eaten can of tuna
> a snowshoe
> algebra homework
> the death of an old uncle

What connections did you establish, and why? Now try the same exercise again but with completely different links.

❷ Link these events in a narrative of 500 words:

> going to the bathroom
> getting thrown out of a bar
> flying a kite
> wiping out when snowboarding
> cooking lasagna for the first time

What is the logic of plot, and what happens when you violate it? When is it permissible to do so, and when not? Now arrange the events in another order. What does that change?

READINGS

Richard Brautigan: "A Need for Gardens"

When I got there they were burying the lion in the back yard again. As usual, it was a hastily dug grave, not really large enough to hold the lion and dug with a maximum of incompetence and they were trying to stuff the lion into a sloppy little hole.

The lion as usual took it quite stoically. Having been buried at least fifty times during the last two years, the lion had gotten used to being buried in the back yard.

I remember the first time they buried him. He didn't know what was happening. He was a younger lion, then, and was frightened and confused, but now he knew what was happening because he was an older lion and had been buried so many times.

He looked vaguely bored as they folded his front paws across his chest and started throwing dirt in his face.

It was basically hopeless. The lion would never fit the hole. It had never fit a hole in the back yard before and it never would. They just couldn't dig a hole big enough to bury that lion in.

"Hello," I said. "The hole's too small."

"Hello," they said. "No, it isn't."

This had been our standard greeting now for two years.

I stood there and watched them for an hour or so struggling desperately to bury the lion, but they were only able to bury ¼ of him before they gave up in disgust and stood around trying to blame each other for not making the hole big enough.

"Why don't you put a garden in next year? I said. "This soil looks like it might grow some good carrots."

They didn't think that was very funny.

(285 WORDS)

DISCUSSION

What's being made fun of, and how? What could burying a lion symbolize? Can even live burial ever become routine? Write your own story with an absurd symbol in the middle.

Donald Barthelme: "The Baby"

The first thing the baby did wrong was to tear pages out of her books. So we made a rule that each time she tore a page out of a book she had to stay alone in her room for four hours, behind the closed door. She was tearing out about a page a day, in the beginning, and the rule worked fairly well, although the crying and screaming from behind the closed door were unnerving. We reasoned that that was the price you had to pay, or part of the price you had to pay. But then as her grip improved she got to tearing out two pages at a time, which meant eight hours alone in her room, behind the closed door, which just doubled the annoyance for everybody. But she wouldn't quit doing it. And then as time went on we began getting days when she tore out three or four pages, which put her alone in her room for as much as sixteen hours at a stretch, interfering with normal feeding and worrying my wife. But I felt that if you made a rule you had to stick to it, had to be consistent, otherwise they get the wrong idea. She was about fourteen months old or fifteen months old at that point. Often, of course, she'd go to sleep, after an hour or so of yelling, that was a mercy. Her room was very nice, with a nice wooden rocking horse and practically a hundred dolls and stuffed animals. Lots of things to do in that room if you used your time wisely, puzzles and things. Unfortunately sometimes when we opened the door we'd find that she'd torn more pages out of more books while she was inside, and these pages had to be added to the total, in fairness.

The baby's name was Born Dancin'. We gave the baby some of our wine, red, white, and blue, and spoke seriously to her. But it didn't do any good.

I must say she got real clever. You'd come up to her where she was playing on the floor, in those rare times when she was out of her room, and there'd be a book there, open beside her, and you'd inspect it and it would look perfectly all right. And then you'd look closely and you'd find a page that had one little corner torn, could easily pass for ordinary wear-and-tear but I knew what she'd done, she'd torn off this little corner and swallowed it. So that had to count and it did. They will go to any lengths to thwart you. My wife said that maybe we were being too rigid and that the baby was losing weight. But I pointed out to her that the baby had a long life to live and had to live in a world with others, had to live in a world where there were many, many rules, and if you couldn't learn to play by the rules you were going to be left out in the cold with no character, shunned and ostracized by everyone. The longest we ever kept her in her room consecutively was eighty-eight hours, and that ended when my wife took the door off its hinges with a crowbar even though the baby still owed us twelve hours because she was working off twenty-five pages. I put the door back on its hinges and added a big lock, one that opened only if you put a magnetic card in a slot, and I kept the card.

But things didn't improve. The baby would come out of her room like a bat out of hell and rush to the nearest book, *Goodnight Moon* or whatever, and begin tearing pages out of it hand over fist. I mean there'd be thirty-four pages of *Goodnight Moon* on the floor in ten seconds. Plus the covers. I began to get a little worried. When I added up her indebtedness, in terms of hours, I could see that she wasn't going to get out of her room until 1992, if then. Also, she was looking pretty wan. She hadn't been to the park in weeks. We had more or less of an ethical crisis on our hands.

I solved it by declaring that it was *all right* to tear pages out of books, and moreover, that it was all right to *have torn* pages out of books in the past. That is one of the satisfying things about being a parent—you've got a lot of moves, each one good as gold. The baby and I sit happily on the floor, side by side, tearing pages out of books, and sometimes, just for fun, we go out on the street and smash a windshield together.

(798 WORDS)

DISCUSSION

What's the absurd premise here, and how does it progress? Are you sympathetic to the baby or the parents? What do you make of the resolution? Can you rewrite this story from the baby's point of view?

What If?

LET'S RETURN to the two main questions for flash fiction: What can you accomplish in a few pages, and how? One way is to sketch a scene as in a vignette, but another approach involves a different way of thinking about what a story does: set up a premise and push it to its logical conclusion. What if everyone could fly with implanted rotors? What if we lived in a dogless world and all of a sudden a poodle appeared? If this approach seems to border on fantasy and science fiction (F&SF), that's no coincidence: Years ago, back in the 1950s, a magazine called *If* arrived on the scene, and during its run of over two decades, it published some of the most notable names in F&SF. Some of the pieces were just long enough to take a premise to its QED conclusion. Their brevity was a virtue, like a geometric proof in which only the necessary steps are listed.

Insert your own "What if?" here. But read some F&SF, or you're likely to come up with a concept that's been done a lot already, including seventeen variations on zombies.

Fantasy and science fiction are, in fact, different fields, even if they seem to share a lot of territory. A working definition of science fiction is the effect of science and technology on society, put into a story. What if a small African village developed a device that could truly think? Before tackling a narrative like this, make sure you do a little research on artificial intelligence: what's out there right now and what might plausibly come within the next few decades. Fantasy, on the other hand, deals with the impossible: dragons, magic. In the land of Yrr, every girl reaching the age of twelve must purge the demon in her soul—or die. As you can see, the setup is key: it's what grabs the audience. Not that fantasy or science fiction isn't interested in character, but the focus includes something larger than individual psychology. The fun of it is in wish fulfillment: people can fly! But in science fiction, you need to pay some attention to the science: avian DNA injected into our pectoral muscles, let's say. In fantasy, we may cast a spell or pray to a bird goddess.

One famous practitioner of the beguiling premise pushed to its limits in a short span is Jorge Luis Borges. Though some of his best-known stories extend beyond the confines of flash fiction, he has written many that fit on a page or two. In "A Dialog About a Dialog," for instance, two voices debate the end of the body and the possible immortality of the soul until the first voice confesses uncertainty over whether they're still living. In "The Two Kings and the Two Labyrinths," Borges recounts the tale of a Babylonian king who has his architects and wizards build him an almost impossibly intricate labyrinth. After an Arabian king nearly perishes inside, the Arabian gets revenge by abducting the Babylonian ruler to the Arabian's native terrain, telling him, "In Babylon you lured me into a labyrinth of brass cluttered with many stairways, doors, and walls; now the Almighty has brought it to pass that I show you mine, which has no stairways to climb, nor doors to force, nor unending galleries to wear one down, nor walls to block one's way" (translated by Andrew Hurley). The Babylonian is left to perish in the desert.

Of course, many provocative premises can be part of our world: What if a hurricane takes away everything you ever owned except the one possession you are most ashamed of? How would you feel if your parents each gained more than two hundred pounds, and what would you do? Here are two ways to proceed:

1   Take a strange premise and carry it to its logical end. Suppose we all grew an extra limb?

2   Take a logical observation to an absurd extreme. Social media are taking up more and more of our time.

Here's a light fantasy in an extremely brief span:

Once upon a time, there was a world in which all wishes came true. It was a lush, green world, with a contented populace, and one man named Don. Don was always wondering why the world was the way it was, and one day he stood up and exclaimed, "I wish there were no more wishes!"

Things are tough all over.

EXERCISES

❶ Take these five premises and develop them within the space of 500 words:

What if the speed of sound slowed down to three miles an hour?
What if cows could talk but otherwise had the same intelligence as always?
What do three prisoners in one cell, all condemned to die the next morning, talk about?
In this society, women can easily overpower the men.
The only way through the village takes you by the sorcerer's hut.

❷ Now come up with your own premise, the more discombobulating, the better. Develop the idea along the lines suggested, but make sure to wrap it up after two pages. Note that some really good premises may be utterly impossible, but for the duration of the story, they sound true. The British poet and essayist Samuel Taylor Coleridge called this effect the "willing suspension of disbelief." It's not the most graceful phrase, but it sums up the reader's experience while engrossed in the story.

READINGS

Wayland Hilton-Young: "The Choice"

Before Williams went into the future he bought a camera and a tape recording machine and learned shorthand. That night, when all was ready,
we made coffee and put out brandy and glasses against his return.

"Good-bye," I said. "Don't stay too long."

"I won't," he answered.

I watched him carefully, and he hardly flickered. He must have made
a perfect landing on the very second he had taken off from. He seemed
not a day older; we had expected he might spend several years away.

"Well?"

"Well," said he, "let's have some coffee."

I poured it out, hardly able to contain my impatience. As I gave it to
him I said again, "Well?"

"Well, the thing is, I can't remember."

"Can't remember? Not a thing?"

He thought for a moment and answered sadly, "Not a thing."

"But your notes? The camera? The recording-machine?"

The notebook was empty, the indicator of the camera rested at "1"
where we had set it, the tape was not even loaded into the recording
machine.

"But good heavens," I protested, "why? How did it happen? Can you
remember nothing at all?"

"I can remember only one thing."

"What was that?"

"I was shown everything, and I was given the choice whether I should
remember it or not after I got back."

"And you chose not to? But what an extraordinary thing to—"

"Isn't it?" he said. "One can't help wondering why."

(235 WORDS)

DISCUSSION

What's frightening about time travel? What do you think the future holds for our society? For our world? Is there anything you'd choose to forget if you could?

Dicky Murphy: "The Magician's Umbrella"

Because he was a magician, people thought he was always doing tricks. But he was much more than a magician (a Lionel train enthusiast, for instance) and so he was not, in fact, always doing tricks. Sometimes he had trouble communicating this. It was hardest on dates, especially when the lady had been selected from the previous night's audience, as was the case with tonight's date.

It bothered him when a date mistook quotidian acts for magic. For one, it made him look like less of a magician. If lighting a cigarette was one of his tricks, then he didn't deserve to call himself a purveyor of magic, no less a prestidigitator par excellence. And furthermore, if the girl saw a trick in everything he did, then soon she would tire of his magic. And then she might miss the finale.

The finale that night was "The Magician's Umbrella." The trick was said to originate somewhere along the Dalmatian coast in the early seventeenth century. Stories said it wasn't even a trick, rather a rain dance gone bad. These stories were, of course, apocryphal, as Dalmatians never danced, least of all for rain.

Debatable origins aside, one thing was clear: The Magician's Umbrella was the hardest trick in the entire world of magic. Only two living magicians had mastered it: one was serving time in Lima, Peru. The other was on a date with a lady from last night's audience.

If you'd been on that street on that night, you might have noticed that the air suddenly stopped like a cheating husband, caught. You might have noticed that the clouds rushed in from the north, south, east, and west, as if drawn by a magnet. If you were on that street, at least one thing's for sure; you'd have gotten wet. Very wet, very quickly.

But not if you were on a date with the magician.

The rain was really ninety-nine percent of the trick, the umbrella just a flourish. But by that point in the evening she'd already applauded his catching of a cab and the pulling out of her chair and even the taking off of her jacket. She giggled when he made wine come out of a bottle and gasped when, from his wallet, he pulled a gold American Express. This late in the date, the young lady was just out of astonishment.

Which is why she didn't bat an eyelash. Not for the umbrella, not even for the rain.

And that's why she never saw the magician again.

She later told friends he simply disappeared, but of course that was just an illusion. At least he left cab fare and tip in her pocket.

(448 WORDS)

DISCUSSION

What's the problem with being a professional magician? Is it like the comedian who makes people laugh just by saying, "How are you?" Since you're a writer, do people expect you to speak literarily or at least tell good stories?

Genre

"Allow me to explain my new gizmatron."

Girl meets boy; girl loses boy; girl gets boy back.

Sound familiar? These are nanofiction capsules of genre fiction, which is to say any narrative that follows a formula, whether it's a western, a mystery, a romance, fantasy, science fiction, horror, and so on. "You can go anywhere you want in the castle, as long as you don't enter the last room on the third floor." You know what's going to happen, right? These are stories with fixed plots, stock characters, and even standard lines. Where do you think "Meanwhile, back at the ranch" came from?

The term *genre*, etymologically related to *genus* and *gender*, used to mean literature of a specific form, as in the epic or the novel. Nowadays, in our age of specialization, we've developed this definition to fit marketing slots, as in, "Over there in the rack by the wall is the mystery section." In the process, the term has acquired a derogatory feel, which is unfortunate, especially since so much of what we write and read is thinly disguised genre fiction. *Literary* fiction, by comparison, devotes too much attention to language and the peculiarities of life to be easily characterized, in which what happens and to whom it happens is not subservient to any conventions per se.

So why should you spend your hard-earned 500–1,000 words repeating well-worn stories? First of all, don't disdain a type of fiction just because it's a type. Most readers like genre stories. The biggest fiction market around is romance. People are comfortable with formulas, though they may eventually want a change or two: a predictable romance plot but this time set in the Australian outback. The same fantasy world of dragons and humans, only in this world, humans breathe fire, and dragons ride them. Maybe you *can* do something with these old ideas. An inventive mind can alter the patterns or at least ring a change or two in an old tune.

Playing with conventions is particularly fruitful in genre flash fiction, where brevity compels you to leave out a lot anyway. And you can save a lot of space by not having to explain what most readers are familiar with, from the old-time saloon to the magic pentagram chalked on the floor. A few well-placed references will establish the formula. Then change an element or how it combines with the whole. But first, as they say in westerns, you have to know the territory.

Take the western, a genre that had its heyday a while ago but which continues to surprise. Here's what doesn't surprise: sharp-shooting cowboys, a mining or ranching town, a whore with a heart of gold, the Last Chance saloon with its swinging doors and a drunk piano player, a sheriff, a deputy, and a gunfight. Your job in a flash fiction western is to push the edge of the envelope—or corral. What about a western that takes place in Maine, or a sheriff who's eighty years old? You have the space for one scene: show what's happened.

Or take mysteries, though they've been somewhat taken over by the thriller genre. Here, the reader solves a crime along with the detective, following logical laws. Witness criminals ingenious beyond belief, love affairs turned into murder plots, and corruption where you least suspected it. Behold the locked-room mystery, a popular subgenre decades ago: How did Professor Rattery hang himself and *then* drink a glass of whisky? In your flash fiction, how about just the wrap-up—in which the solver is complicit in the crime or in which no solution is possible? Find a convention and bend it.

Science fiction, or SF, is an omnivorous genre come of age. The plot hinges on some aspect of science or technology. Someone invents a time machine. But what if, ten years later, everyone has a time machine? Because of a plague, everyone loses the ability to speak. And you thought we texted a lot now! Note the double trend in SF: amazing, enabling scientific advances—or the devastating effects of technology. See the "What If?" chapter for more examples.

You might also try your hand at romance, but try to avoid the usual girl-meets-boy scenarios. Think interspecies, think multiple partners, think of how complicated love is, and focus on one facet in 1,000 words. At least change the locale (see the "Setting" chapter, and arrange a tryst underwater).

Other genres include fantasy: SF without the science, as in the subgenre S&S, or sword and sorcery. Think magic, strange creatures, and unearthly physical attributes, like the ability to be in two places at once. And what about horror? Finish your flash fiction piece before the laptop monster arises from the keyboard and sucks you in.

Here are some tips on how to be original, or at least a little different, in genre flash fiction:

Come up with an idea that hasn't been done yet. You're wrong. That was done fifteen years ago. But how about changing the sexes, the era, or the location?

Merge ideas: a western set on the moon, a romance between computers, or a horror love story? Been there, done that—so keep trying. Recombination is an art.

If the ideas are old, reanimate them with some real characters in place of plot-driven mannequins. In this world, people move as slowly as snails, but your protagonist is kind of a slow person, and that's okay with her. Maybe she meets a guy even slower than she is.

EXERCISES

❶ Start in a programmatic genre pattern, then break the pattern with a character who won't get with the program.

❷ Merge two genres.

READINGS

Roxane Gay: "The Mistress of Baby Breath"

When I find little babies left alone by their mothers, I take them and kiss them until their bright baby eyes shine with laughter, with joy. I carefully tuck the little babies into my gossamer-lined pockets. I go on with my day, looking in on old friends, walking by the water and throwing in stones. While I am walking with little babies in my gossamer-lined pockets, I crush rose petals until they bleed, until their essence snakes around and stains my fingers a serious shade of red. Then I give the little babies my rose-infused fingers to play with. I often giggle because one of my pocket babies is always nipping at my fingers with a moist, gummy mouth.

At night, I lay the little babies on a soft pallet or set them in a sock drawer. They squirm happily, rolling over and around one another, a humming, fleshy tangle of warm, powdered, sweet baby parts. After I feed them honey and milk, after I pat their backs and trace the fragile landscape of their new infant spines, I collect their baby breath in sachets of silk and store my treasure in a locked glass case for safekeeping.

I fall asleep listening to the little babies coo contentedly. Once in a while they will stir, or cry for the mothers that left them alone, the mothers who held them to their warm breasts and nourished them wholly. In these moments, I cradle these babies in my arms, nipping their foreheads between my teeth and folding the rolls of their chubby baby thighs.

Each morning, I send their mothers kind and generous notes written in dark ink on bright and heavy linen paper. I tell their mothers about how their babies smile, and how their babies' cheeks are plump and delicious and how I drink cream from their dimpled thighs with my soft widow's lips. I wrap the notes into tight scrolls, put them in glass bottles. I tie the bottles to brightly colored kites and throw them into the wind.

When I have to leave my boxcar to attend to my day, I dress the little babies in matching plaid jumpers and matching plaid hats to protect their thin baby skin and the tender bone of their soft baby skulls. I tickle their feet and the fat palms of their hands. I feed them dandelion wine and little balls of fresh sugary dough. Just before setting out, I hang the babies on strong copper hooks set close enough that they can reach out and hold each other's hands. While I'm gone, the little babies will furiously kick their stubby little legs so that they can swing closer to one another. They will tell each other baby secrets and sing sad, mysterious songs.

When I'm not gathering little babies from the mothers, I sell fresh baby breath from a roadside stand with honey milk, strange fruit and other useful goods. All day long, passersby want the secret of my sweet baby breath. I smile and tell them the truth. I sing a lullaby about stolen little babies, smelling sweet, smiling wide. I sing about how they're all holding hands, drunk on wine, dangling from strong copper hooks. When my lullaby is done, the passersby laugh. They are charmed and they press cool silver coins into my larcenous widow's hands.

(558 WORDS)

DISCUSSION

Does this piece qualify as horror or fantasy or both? What happens to the babies? What's the motive of the speaker, and what's her tone? How should we as readers react?

Tara Orchard: "My Love"

"I love you. No—please don't interrupt me." She places her finger over his lips, as if to keep him quiet. Staring at his lips as if they held the solution to everything bad in her life, she traces them with her thin fingers. Lightly. Gently. A whisper gliding across the thin bottom lip. A sigh slipping over the almost invisible top lip. "You mean everything to me."

She tilts her head to the side, smiling soothingly with tenderness and adoration. Her dark fingers sweep up his pale face and stop at his temple so she can cup his cheek with her slightly callused palm. A soft groan escapes the confines of her mouth. "You don't know what you do to me. I . . . I've never felt this way before, and I can't keep hiding what you are to me. I need to tell you—. Stop. I can't think when you look at me like that." She shakes her head gently. "If I stop, I'm not sure I'll be able to continue, and I need you to know how I feel. It's eating me alive."

She caresses his cheek with her thumb, then runs her hand through his shoulder-length light blond hair. Her hand gets caught on a knot, but she makes quick work of detangling it. She leans over and nuzzles right behind his ear. The gentle waves of his hair tickle her cheek, but she doesn't move. She takes a deep breath in, trying to memorize his scent. "You smell so good. You always do. Your smell reminds me of home. Musky, with just a touch of bitterness.

"I know you get jealous." She trails her nose across his cheek and stops right next to his, leaning forward to rest her forehead on his. "But those guys are friends. That's it. I could never love them the way I love you." She grazes his lips with hers. "You have nothing to worry about. . . . I could never hurt you like that. It would be like trying to hurt the other half of my soul.

"It's like I have an open wound that throbs when I'm not with you, constantly reminding me that I'm not where I should be. I spend all my time away from you, thinking about what excuse I can come up with to come back. To be by your side, touching your smooth white skin and seeing those expressive and beautiful light blue eyes. Headaches, stomach bugs, one-day viruses, my cat's sick, my cat died, anything. Anything to see you again."

She places her hands on his cheeks, so gently, and she sighs. "I have to go. You should get some rest. I'll be back as soon as I can but, with everyone on the lookout for anything suspicious, it'll be hard." She lifts his head off the table and carries it back over to the black refrigerator against the wall. She cradles him in the curve of her arm as she opens the door, revealing five more heads. All blond. All male. All howling soundlessly, mouths frozen open and blue eyes stuck wide open in terror and surprise.

She kisses his lips softly and places him in the empty spot of the top shelf. Her fingers trail over the side of his face once more. "Stay safe, my love. I'll be back as soon as I can. And maybe I'll even bring my new friend." She waves as she closes the door. She presses a button on the wall next to it and the fridge sinks back into the wall until all that is left is an empty space and a barren wall. She grabs her keys off the table that his head had been resting on, and jogs up the rusting basement stairs.

(627 WORDS)

DISCUSSION

Where do the two genres of romance and horror merge? Could the blend occur at some other juncture? How would the piece be different with an appalled attitude?

Setting

THE PASTURE IS IN THE BACK of an abandoned farm off CR 403, smelling faintly of vanished hay. In the noonday heat, the cicadas are chirping from an invisible grandstand. The tree under which Jeff and Leo hold their picnic is a gigantic sycamore that looks like a holdover from prehistoric days. Its shiny leaves are big as fans, and when a susurrus rises, it's as if they're being cooled by a horde of green slaves. Next to their blanket, looming like a wall, the trunk has three sets of initials inscribed, but the bark has grown over the marks, and the only clear form that remains is a warped heart.

Think of a setting piece as a character sketch of a place, ideal for a short space. It's an exercise in observation, but intelligent examination is selective and makes judgments. The picnic previously described seems like a significant event, but what the reader really notices and recalls long after finishing the piece is the setting, namely, that tree. What energizes the prose is the description: the way the branches hover thick as a ceiling or how the root flanking the blanket is like a giant's knuckle. Good description isn't just a flurry of adjectives but also rich imagery, metaphors, sensory information, and speculations. What kind of bird is that on the far branch, eying Leo as if he were a fat worm? Ending on that note turns the setting into a miniature story.

Setting is important in any piece of fiction where it impinges on the plot or characters: if we ever get out of this desert alive . . . But as the ignored poor relation in much of fiction writing, it can also be the main event if done right. In historical fiction, such as a crime set in 17th-century China, it can be a key player: Look at the marketplace and what's being sold there. Is that curvy piece of metal a dagger? What are the vendors calling out? What's that smell? End right there.

The setting needn't be exotic, and in fact a good writer may extract more interest from the local McDonald's—a ketchup stain in the shape of a crying face—than in the low red banquettes of some more regal establishment. The joy is in the details, as microscopic as you like. Not just a seat near the back of the restaurant but a booth where the red vinyl has been patched with an X of duct tape and the Formica tabletop is ever so slightly crooked. The music playing—is that a cover of the Bee Gees?

Where you set your action can make a difference in the plot. Think about a case of murder in the Antarctic, where there's no place to escape and the corpse that the criminal has tried to hide won't decompose in the frigid climate. A setting involves conditions and limits and sometimes surprises. In Robert Heinlein's short short story "Columbus Was a Dope," the last line of dialogue marks the climax and the point of the story: the action takes place on the moon.

But suppose you're not the kind of person who notices what poster is hanging in the bathroom or what the door knocker looks like. You can work on the art of noticing. What do you pick up as you walk along the corridor to class? What do you smell when you hit the cafeteria? Our sense of sight is so primary that "I see" is tantamount to "I understand," but that doesn't mean you should neglect sound, touch, taste, or smell. Or invent your own sense, some other way to apprehend the world.

Beyond mere sensory data are metaphorical comparisons. The dead writer's desk is an old aircraft carrier, where aging manuscripts have landed, never to take off again. The kitchen table, with its missing chair, represents a children's game where someone won't get to sit. The noonday sun is a giant's eye. Metaphor adds dimension and scope to what otherwise is just a desk, a table, or a sunny day. And since it's too easy to borrow metaphors old as the hills, make up some of your own.

As long as you're naming parts of the landscape, you should also learn the nomenclature. What's a brume, and what's a butte? If the setting involves a moving van, what's the word for the wheeled thingamajig that you can load boxes on? (A hand truck.) What's a last in the shoemaker's old shop, or a CPU at the computer store? Know what you're talking about, and convey that information. It's what local color is all about, and it makes you a reliable guide to the territory.

How does all this work in a flash fiction devoted to setting? Focus on the background while keeping the action simple. Characters come and go, but the landscape abides. Even the wooden stage outlasts the actors. After you've elaborated on seven planks and the creaks they make, have your character perform one action and exit, stage left.

Here's a sum-up of advice for flash fiction devoted to setting:

ONE TIP: Don't focus just on the visuals, but also include sounds and other sensory data. Where does that pinging come from?

ANOTHER TIP: Don't be static in your description. Show how your setting breathes, even if it's just a lawn.

A THIRD TIP: Describe your setting through metaphors and analogies, particularly of size, color, and shape. That tree is as small as a hunched-over old man.

A FOURTH TIP: Take one small spot and look closer and closer at it until it yields intriguing patterns. Why does that wallpaper design cut off right at the seventh circle?

A FIFTH TIP: Change the context. It's a seven-story building—in the middle of a cornfield.

A SIXTH TIP: Insert one last observation about the place that pulls everything else into perspective. That dull red patch is blood.

THE SEVENTH TIP: Exotic locales are alluring, but finding what's salient in the familiar is a subtle art well worth cultivating. What aspects of this building make it home?

EXERCISES

❶ Create a setting that uses all five senses, and add a sixth sense at the end.

❷ Too many settings are nonmoving. Create a setting with only action verbs.

READINGS

Bharati Mukherjee: "Courtly Vision"

Jahanara Begum stands behind a marble grille in her palace at Fatehpur-Sikri.

Count Barthelmy, an adventurer from beyond frozen oceans, crouches in a lust-darkened arbor. His chest—a tear-shaped fleck of rust—lifts away from the gray, flat trunk of a mango tree. He is swathed in the coarse, quaint clothes of his cool-weather country. Jacket, pantaloons, shawl, swell and cave in ardent pleats. He holds a peacock's feather to his lips. His face is colored in admonitory pink. The feather is dusty aqua, broken-spined. His white-gloved hand pillows a likeness of the Begum, painted on a grain of rice by Basawan, the prized court artist. Two red-eyed parrots gouge the patina of grass at the adventurer's feet; their buoyant, fluffy breasts caricature the breasts of Moghul virgins. The Count is posed full-front; the self-worshipful body of a man who has tamed thirteen rivers and seven seas. Dainty thighs bulge with wayward expectancy. The head twists savagely upward at an angle unreckoned except in death, anywhere but here. In profile the lone prismatic eye betrays the madman and insomniac.

On the terrace of Jahanara Begum's palace, a slave girl kneels; her forearms, starry with jewels, strain toward the fluted handle of a decanter. Two bored eunuchs squat on their fleshy haunches, awaiting their wine. Her simple subservience hints at malevolent dreams, of snake venom rubbed into wine cups or daggers concealed between young breasts, and the eunuchs are menaced, their faces pendulous with premonition.

In her capacious chamber the Begum waits, perhaps for death from the serving-girl, for ravishing, or merely the curtain of fire from the setting sun. The chamber is open on two sides, the desert breeze stiffens her veil into a gauzy disc. A wild peacock, its fanned-out feathers beaten back by the same breeze, cringes on the bit of marble floor visible behind her head. Around the Begum, retainers conduct their inefficient chores. One, her pursed navel bare, slackens her grip on a *morchal* of plumes; another stumbles, biceps clenched, under the burden of a golden hookah bowl studded with translucent rubies and emeralds; a third stoops, her back an eerie, writhing arc, to straighten a low table littered with cosmetics in jewelled pillboxes. The Begum is a tall, rigid figure as she stands behind a marble grille. From her fists, which she holds in front of her like tiny shields, sprouts a closed, upright lotus bloom. Her gaze slips upward, past the drunken gamblers on the roof-terraces, to the skyline where fugitive cranes pass behind a blue cloud.

Oh, beauteous and beguiling Begum, has your slave-girl apprised the Count of the consequences of a night of bliss?

Under Jahanara Begum's window, in a courtyard cooled with fountains into whose basin slaves have scattered rose petals, sit Fathers Aquaviva and Henriques, ingenuous Portuguese priests. They have dogged the emperor through inclement scenery. Now they pause in the emperor's famed, new capital, eyes closed, abstemious hands held like ledges over their brows to divert the sullen desert breeze. Their faces seem porous; the late afternoon has slipped through the skin and distended the chins and cheeks. Before their blank, radiant gazes, seven itinerant jugglers heap themselves into a shuddering pyramid. A courtier sits with the priests on a divan covered with brocaded silk. He too is blind to the courage of gymnasts. He is distracted by the wondrous paintings the priests have spread out on the arabesques of the rugs at their feet. Mother and Child. Child and Mother. The Moghul courier—child of Islam, ruler of Hindus—finds the motif repetitive. What comforting failure of the imagination these priests are offering. What precarious boundaries set on life's playful fecundity. He hears the Fathers murmur. They are devising stratagems on a minor scale. They want to trick the emperor into kissing Christ, who on each somber canvas is a bright, white, healthy baby. The giant figures seem to him simple and innocuous, not complicated and infuriating like the Hindu icons hidden in the hills. In the meantime his eyes draw comfort from the unclad angels who watch over the Madonna to protect her from heathens like him. Soft-fleshed, flying women. He will order the court artists to paint him a harem of winged women on a single poppy seed.

The emperor will not kiss Christ tonight. He is at the head of his army, riding a piebald horse out of his new walled city. He occupies the foreground of that agate-colored paper, a handsome young man in a sun-yellow *jama*. Under the *jama* his shoulders pulsate to the canny violent rhythm of his mount. Behind him in a thick choking diagonal stream follow his soldiers. They scramble and spill on the sandy terrain; spiky desert grass slashes their jaunty uniforms of muslin. Tiny, exhilarated profiles crowd the battlements. In the women's palace, tinier figures flit from patterned window grille, to grille. The citizens have begun to celebrate. Grandfathers leading children by the wrists are singing of the emperor's victories over invisible rebels. Shopkeepers, coy behind their taut paunches, give away their syrupy sweets. Even the mystics with their haggard, numinous faces have allowed themselves to be distracted by yet another parade.

So the confident emperor departs.

The Moghul evening into which he drags his men with the promise of unimaginable satisfactions is grayish gold with the late afternoon, winter light. It spills down the rims of stylized rocks that clog the high horizon. The light is charged with unusual excitement and it discovers the immense intimacy of darkness, the erotic shadowiness of the cave-deep arbor in which the Count crouches and waits. The foliage of the mango tree yields sudden, bountiful shapes. Excessive, unruly life—monkeys, serpents, herons, thieves naked to the waist—bloom and burgeon on its branches. The thieves, their torsos pushing through clusters of leaves, run rapacious fingers on their dagger blades.

They do not discern the Count. The Count does not overhear the priests. Adventurers all, they guard from each other the common courtesy of their subterfuge. They sniff the desert air and the air seems full of portents. In the remote horizon three guards impale three calm, emaciated men. Behind the low wall of a *namaz* platform, two courtiers quarrel, while a small boy sneaks up and unties their horses. A line of stealthy women prostrate themselves and pray at the doorways of a temple in a patch of browning foliage. Over all these details float three elegant whorls of cloud, whorls in the manner of Chinese painting, imitated diligently by men who long for rain.

The emperor leaves his capital, applauded by flatterers and loyal citizens. Just before riding off the tablet's edge into enemy territory, he twists back on his saddle and shouts a last-minute confidence to his favorite court-painter. He is caught in reflective profile, the quarter-arc of his mustache suggests a man who had permitted his second thoughts to confirm his spontaneous judgment.

Give me total vision, commands the emperor. His voice hisses above the hoarse calls of the camels. *You, Basawan, who can paint my Begum on a grain of rice, see what you can do with the infinite vistas the size of my opened hand. Hide nothing from me, my co-wanderer. Tell me how my new capital will fail, will turn to dust and these marbled terraces be home to jackals and infidels. Tell me who to fear and who to kill but tell it to me in a way that makes me smile. Transport me through dense fort walls and stone grilles and into the hearts of men.*

"Emperor on Horseback Leaves Walled City"
Painting on Paper, 24 cms x 25.8 cms
Painter Unknown. No superscription
c. 1584 A.D.
Lot No. SLM 4027-66
Est. Price $750

(1,291 WORDS)

DISCUSSION

An ekphrasis is a piece of writing about a work of art. Does this piece extend the painting and, if so, how? What can you do in writing that you can't in painting and vice versa?

Alice Walker: "The Flowers"

It seemed to Myop as she skipped lightly from hen house to pigpen to smokehouse that the days had never been as beautiful as these. The air held a keenness that made her nose twitch. The harvesting of the corn and cotton, peanuts and squash, made each day a golden surprise that caused excited little tremors to run up her jaws.

Myop carried a short, knobby stick. She struck out at random at chickens she liked, and worked out the beat of a song on the fence around the pigpen. She felt light and good in the warm sun. She was ten, and nothing existed for her but her song, the stick clutched in her dark brown hand, and the tat-de-ta-ta-ta of accompaniment.

Turning her back on the rusty boards of her family's sharecropper cabin, Myop walked along the fence till it ran into the stream made by the spring. Around the spring, where the family got drinking water, silver ferns and wildflowers grew. Along the shallow banks pigs rooted. Myop watched the tiny white bubbles disrupt the thin black scale of soil and the water that silently rose and slid away down the stream.

She had explored the woods behind the house many times. Often, in late autumn, her mother took her to gather nuts among the fallen leaves. Today she made her own path, bouncing this way and that way, vaguely keeping an eye out for snakes. She found, in addition to various common but pretty ferns and leaves, an armful of strange blue flowers with velvety ridges and a sweetsuds bush full of the brown, fragrant buds.

By twelve o'clock, her arms laden with sprigs of her findings, she was a mile or more from home. She had often been as far before, but the strangeness of the land made it not as pleasant as her usual haunts. It seemed gloomy in the little cove in which she found herself. The air was damp, the silence close and deep.

Myop began to circle back to the house, back to the peacefulness of the morning. It was then she stepped smack into his eyes. Her heel became lodged in the broken ridge between brow and nose, and she reached down quickly, unafraid, to free herself. It was only when she saw his naked grin that she gave a little yelp of surprise.

He had been a tall man. From feet to neck covered a long space. His head lay beside him. When she pushed back the leaves and layers of earth and debris Myop saw that he'd had large white teeth, all of them cracked or broken, long fingers, and very big bones. All his clothes had rotted away except some threads of blue denim from his overalls. The buckles of the overalls had turned green.

Myop gazed around the spot with interest. Very near where she'd stepped into the head was a wild pink rose. As she picked it to add to her bundle she noticed a raised mound, a ring, around the rose's root. It was the rotted remains of a noose, a bit of shredding plowline, now blending benignly into the soil. Around an overhanging limb of a great spreading oak clung another piece. Frayed, rotted, bleached, and frazzled—barely there—but spinning restlessly in the breeze. Myop laid down her flowers.

And the summer was over.

(562 WORDS)

DISCUSSION

What does the setting show on the surface, and what does it reveal? Can a setting be innocent, or is that feeling always our own projection? How does a heinous racial incident get compressed into so few words?

Twists

READERS LIKE SURPRISES IN STORIES. The bad girl performs a good deed, or the lively gentleman turns out to be a ghost. You thought the plot was as predictable as the sunrise or the character would always back up his companion. You were wrong, yet when you reread the story, you realize that the clues were there all along. The bad girl always had a soft spot for her aunt. The gentleman looked vaguely transparent in the mirror. Such stories work by a form of misdirection, in which the author constructs the setup so that the appearance masks the reality. At the end of the story, the mask is pulled off, and voilà! Because many such stories consist simply of a setup and a disclosure, they're ideal for the flash fiction treatment. Fantasy and science-fiction twist tales abound, for instance, since they deal with an unknown factor or two. But unexpected reversals can occur anytime.

How does a twist story make you feel? Though a twist may be horrifying (what you thought was candy was actually poison), it's almost always satisfying on some level. At the moment of clarity, the reader thinks, *Aha! Now I get it*. Sometimes the character is a victim of situational irony, in which what occurs is the opposite of what should happen. Vicky studies so hard for the bar exam that she overthinks all the questions and fails the test. Sometimes the result may be humorous:

"You told me to kiss Robert Edwards! You mean, there are *two* men in the room named Robert Edwards?" Or the effect may be fatal: Stan, a veteran NASCAR driver and winner of more than fifty races, dies in a parking-lot collision. If you're one of those who feel that life itself is a situational irony, you can come up with a few setups yourself. People may not like a real-life twist, especially if it's unpleasant, but if it happens to someone else—a definition of the reader's experience—then maybe it's okay. It may even be fun.

Most twists have something of the jack-in-the-box about them, popping out at the end. But a really good twist story makes the reader want to go back and reread, to see where the tip-off was hidden, or just to savor the way the narrative was put together. If you come up with a great idea for a twist story, fine, but invest some real effort in the writing so that the sentences themselves, and not just where they lead, are a pleasure. Remember to include salient details, which include close observation and imagery. Make sure that your characters are vibrant, which means making them more than puppets acting out the plot twist. Many story twists could have played out otherwise if it weren't for a character flaw.

Many famous short stories have unexpected endings: De Maupassant's "The Necklace" ("La parure"), for instance, though it's the length of two pieces of flash fiction, and O. Henry's "The Gift of the Magi," which weighs in at more than 2,000 words. O. Henry, whose real name was William Porter, was a master at twist endings: crooks kidnap a child only to find him so obnoxious that they end up paying the parents to take him back ("The Ransom of Red Chief"); a bum who breaks the law every winter to land in a warm jail cell vows to reform— at which point he's arrested ("The Cop and the Anthem"). The British author Hector Hugh Munro, known as Saki, was another well-known practitioner of the form. In "Sredni Vashtar," for instance, a sickly child gains revenge on his overbearing guardian by exploiting her impulse to interfere. "Dusk," a story about a man approached by someone who seems like a panhandler, features a double twist. See below for another of Saki's stories, "The Open Window."

Seemingly so easy in execution, the twist story does have some pit-falls. Overobvious setups are an issue. You don't want readers claiming that they guessed the ending after the first paragraph. Another issue is contrived endings: "C'mon, that would never happen!" Because character development can take a while, flash fiction with a twist tends to be plot-driven: the devastating tornado reunites two families; the woman I swore never to see again accidentally saves my life. But character may also prevail: the lunatic turns out to be the only sane man in town. Just beware triumphs of plot over character, in which the author shoves his people into a resolution that's absurd, given the individuals in the story. She's been selfish her whole life, yet she suddenly turns into a nice person just because someone's nice to her? Remember, a proper twist is prepared for; it only looks spontaneous.

EXERCISES

❶ Here are five situations:

running after the man who stole your backpack
buying a toy at a garage sale
burning dinner to get back at your lover
playing hide-and-seek with your grandchild
promoting your assistant at work

Choose one. What could go wrong? Now save the situation with a reversal.

❷ Double-twist stories are harder to pull off than simple twist tales. Just when the surprise comes, overturning all expectations, another unexpected development pops out, either reversing the first ending or adding an unexpected dimension. Try it. To keep your double-twist story manageable in a short space, stick to one simple problem.

READINGS

Luisa Valenzuela: "Vision Out of the Corner of One Eye"

TRANSLATED BY HELEN LANE

It's true, he put his hand on my ass and I was about to scream bloody murder when the bus passed by a church and he crossed himself. He's a good sort after all, I said to myself. Maybe he didn't do it on purpose or maybe his right hand didn't know what his left hand was up to. I tried to move farther back in the bus—searching for explanations is one thing and letting yourself be pawed is another—but more passengers got on and there was no way I could do it. My wiggling to get out of his reach only let him get a better hold on me and even fondle me. I was nervous and finally moved over. He moved over, too. We passed by another church but he didn't notice it and when he raised his hand to his face it was to wipe the sweat off his forehead. I watched him out of a corner of one eye, pretending that nothing was happening, or at any rate not making him think I liked it. It was impossible to move any farther and he started jiggling me. I decided to get even and put my hand on his behind. A few blocks later I got separated from him by a bunch of people. Then I was swept along by the passengers getting off the bus and now I'm sorry I lost him so suddenly because there was only 7,400 pesos in his wallet and I'd have gotten more out of him if we'd been alone. He seemed affectionate. And very generous.

(265 WORDS)

DISCUSSION

How does your view of the narrator change at two different junctures in the story? Do two wrongs make a right here? Note that one action's canceling another is how many twist stories function.

Saki: "The Open Window"

"My aunt will be down presently, Mr. Nuttel," said a very self-possessed young lady of fifteen; "in the meantime you must try and put up with me."

Framton Nuttel endeavoured to say the correct something which should duly flatter the niece of the moment without unduly discounting the aunt that was to come. Privately he doubted more than ever whether these formal visits on a succession of total strangers would do much towards helping the nerve cure which he was supposed to be undergoing.

"I know how it will be," his sister had said when he was preparing to migrate to this rural retreat; "you will bury yourself down there and not speak to a living soul, and your nerves will be worse than ever from moping. I shall just give you letters of introduction to all the people I know there. Some of them, as far as I can remember, were quite nice."

Framton wondered whether Mrs. Sappleton, the lady to whom he was presenting one of the letters of introduction, came into the nice division.

"Do you know many of the people round here?" asked the niece, when she judged that they had had sufficient silent communion.

"Hardly a soul," said Framton. "My sister was staying here, at the rectory, you know, some four years ago, and she gave me letters of introduction to some of the people here."

He made the last statement in a tone of distinct regret.

"Then you know practically nothing about my aunt?" pursued the self-possessed young lady.

"Only her name and address," admitted the caller. He was wondering whether Mrs. Sappleton was in the married or widowed state. An undefinable something about the room seemed to suggest masculine habitation.

"Her great tragedy happened just three years ago," said the child; "that would be since your sister's time."

"Her tragedy?" asked Framton; somehow in this restful country spot tragedies seemed out of place.

"You may wonder why we keep that window wide open on an October afternoon," said the niece, indicating a large French window that opened on to a lawn.

"It is quite warm for the time of the year," said Framton; "but has that window got anything to do with the tragedy?"

"Out through that window, three years ago to a day, her husband and her two young brothers went off for their day's shooting. They never came back. In crossing the moor to their favourite snipe-shooting ground they were all three engulfed in a treacherous piece of bog. It had been that dreadful wet summer, you know, and places that were safe in other years gave way suddenly without warning. Their bodies were never recovered. That was the dreadful part of it." Here the child's voice lost its self-possessed note and became falteringly human. "Poor aunt always thinks that they will come back someday, they and the little brown spaniel that was lost with them, and walk in at that window just as they used to do. That is why the window is kept open every evening till it is quite dusk. Poor dear aunt, she has often told me how they went out, her husband with his white waterproof coat over his arm, and Ronnie, her youngest brother, singing, 'Bertie, why do you bound?' as he always did to tease her, because she said it got on her nerves. Do you know, sometimes on still, quiet evenings like this, I almost get a creepy feeling that they will all walk in through that window—"

She broke off with a little shudder. It was a relief to Framton when the aunt bustled into the room with a whirl of apologies for being late in making her appearance.

"I hope Vera has been amusing you?" she said.

"She has been very interesting," said Framton.

"I hope you don't mind the open window," said Mrs. Sappleton briskly; "my husband and brothers will be home directly from shooting, and they always come in this way. They've been out for snipe in the marshes today, so they'll make a fine mess over my poor carpets. So like you men-folk, isn't it?"

She rattled on cheerfully about the shooting and the scarcity of birds, and the prospects for duck in the winter. To Framton, it was all purely horrible. He made a desperate but only partially successful effort to turn the talk on to a less ghastly topic, he was conscious that his hostess was giving him only a fragment of her attention, and her eyes were constantly straying past him to the open window and the lawn beyond. It was certainly an unfortunate coincidence that he should have paid his visit on this tragic anniversary.

"The doctors agree in ordering me complete rest, an absence of mental excitement, and avoidance of anything in the nature of violent physical exercise," announced Framton, who laboured under the tolerably widespread delusion that total strangers and chance acquaintances are hungry for the least detail of one's ailments and infirmities, their cause and cure. "On the matter of diet they are not so much in agreement," he continued.

"No?" said Mrs. Sappleton, in a voice which only replaced a yawn at the last moment. Then she suddenly brightened into alert attention—but not to what Framton was saying.

"Here they are at last!" she cried. "Just in time for tea, and don't they look as if they were muddy up to the eyes!"

Framton shivered slightly and turned towards the niece with a look intended to convey sympathetic comprehension. The child was staring out through the open window with dazed horror in her eyes. In a chill shock of nameless fear Framton swung round in his seat and looked in the same direction.

In the deepening twilight three figures were walking across the lawn towards the window, they all carried guns under their arms, and one of them was additionally burdened with a white coat hung over his shoulders. A tired brown spaniel kept close at their heels. Noiselessly they neared the house, and then a hoarse young voice chanted out of the dusk: "I said, Bertie, why do you bound?"

Framton grabbed wildly at his stick and hat; the hall-door, the gravel-drive, and the front gate were dimly noted stages in his headlong retreat. A cyclist coming along the road had to run into the hedge to avoid imminent collision.

"Here we are, my dear," said the bearer of the white mackintosh, coming in through the window, "fairly muddy, but most of it's dry. Who was that who bolted out as we came up?"

"A most extraordinary man, a Mr. Nuttel," said Mrs. Sappleton; "could only talk about his illnesses, and dashed off without a word of good-bye or apology when you arrived. One would think he had seen a ghost."

"I expect it was the spaniel," said the niece calmly; "he told me he had a horror of dogs. He was once hunted into a cemetery somewhere on the banks of the Ganges by a pack of pariah dogs, and had to spend the night in a newly dug grave with the creatures snarling and grinning and foaming just above him. Enough to make anyone lose their nerve."

Romance at short notice was her speciality.

(1,209 WORDS)

DISCUSSION

What makes the niece's lie believable? Is lying just another definition of art? What's the best lie you've ever been told?

Two Viewpoints

ONE OF THE OLDEST SETUPS for a conflict is to present two characters in discussion, first her view, then his. "We need to talk," she starts out.

His response: "I don't have time for this right now."

"You always say that."

"Maybe you have bad timing."

"Really? Is that what you told your last girlfriend?"

"What's that supposed to mean?"

"Is that what you told what's-her-name last night?"

"What? We were just discussing the election."

"Really? Is that why you had your arm around her?"

"But you weren't even—wait, how do you know that?"

As you can hear, two viewpoints can quickly add up to an implied narrative. As for the pacing of such an exchange, think of "contrapuntal," a music word that involves a relationship between two voices, similar in sound yet different in rhythm. Keep it short, especially since quarrels tend to repeat themselves. Continue the exchange as long as it takes to establish a pattern, ending on a note of conclusion, defeat, inalterable difference, or wherever your own conversations take you.

On to subject: What are they discussing or, better, since drama is based on conflict, arguing about? Maybe it's an old topic, inherent in character or situation: twelve years we've been married, and all we do on Fridays is sit at home. Maybe it's something new and alarming: our son, a bright student, is flunking out of college. Or subtle yet sinister: a bad habit of hers, talking too long on the phone, conceals what she's really doing, making drug deals.

Other considerations: How does the exchange begin? With the subject of buying a new carpet? What behavior or remark sets it off? He can't stand her perpetual preference for royal blue. Why and how does it escalate rather than dying down? Last time, she got her way—not this time. How about making it his turn? What's the emotional height, and where should it come in the story? Does he bring up all the times she's had her way and that he's finally had enough?

Bear in mind that a two-viewpoints piece of flash fiction is rooted not just in a situation but also in character. Do the two play well together? Perhaps their conversation is like a ping-pong game, but an uneven one, where one player slams the other's lobs or puts spin on the volleys. One character may be gabby, the other terse. At least try not to have them talk the same. You are how you speak, both in subject and style. That's how you can recognize someone from across a crowded room. A ten-year-old girl from Mississippi speaks differently from an eighty-year-old man from Toronto, in word choice, syntax, and rhythm, among other ways. Culture and class also play important roles. So does mood.

As you progress in your two-viewpoint sketch, pay attention to individual words. Why does the term *free time* keep coming up? What effect does repetition have? Note that to repeat isn't just to echo but to emphasize, to become tiresome, or to impute new meaning through sheer stress. The third time she repeats herself, she means something different, and maybe he picks up on it, and maybe he doesn't.

If it's not all straight dialogue, or even if it is, try not to make it two talking heads. People often move around when they speak, engage in body language, and so on, gestures that can reveal or conceal as much as conversation. And if you're dealing only with what she says and he says, you can still build action into the sentences: "Don't walk away from me when I'm talking to you." "I hate it when you shrug like that."

Where does an argument end? When it's resolved, or just when the participants are exhausted or have exhausted the topic? Or do you get the feeling that this'll happen again tomorrow? All these issues have bearing on the shape of flash fiction devoted to viewpoint.

Must it always be she-he? What about two guys arguing over where to get the best burger, or two women in a committed relationship discussing who should move into whose apartment?

Since this is the 21st century, consider transcripts of telephone calls, Skyping, instant messaging, and voicemail. During a phone call, few speakers have the organizational skill to form long, balanced sentences that build. In texting, people type impulsively, at speed. Think of what those shifts will do to the sentence structure or how texters have come up with new abbreviations and slang (lol).

Don't forget perspective and humor. What may seem terribly important to the participants may appear trivial to anyone listening in. And sometimes, in the middle of the most tempestuous dialogue comes an unintended joke or reversal, and the two people smile in spite of themselves. The reader smiles, too.

"If you weren't so darned stubborn, we wouldn't be having this argument."

"If I weren't so stubborn, I wouldn't still be married to you."

EXERCISES

❶ Sometimes more than two people are involved in a conflict. Try a trio or more, maybe at a party. How do you distinguish among three or more people, especially in a small space? Give them specific props or attributes: the blond guy, the woman with a bad manicure.

Bonus: start an argument that veers into different territory, from who has to take out the dog to the topic of longevity. Double bonus: construct the alternating viewpoints through one voice alone, acknowledging the other while also building his own case.

❷ Tired of human bickering? Try a tree versus the wind, or a bicycle versus a truck.

READINGS

**Robert Schipits: "Dialogue Between Two Teenagers,
One Interested in Cars and One Not"**

Interested: Whose car do you think is faster, yours or mine?

Not Interested: I have no idea.

Interested: Well, okay, what kind of car do you drive?

Not Interested: A 1988 Honda Accord.

Interested: That car is a big piece of shit!

Not Interested: That is what I can afford.

Interested: So, it is still a big piece of shit.

Not Interested: Well, it works.

Interested: Works like a big piece of shit works.

Not Interested: What does that even mean?

[Long pause.]

Interested: You know what kind of car I drive?

Not Interested: No.

Interested: A 1999 Ford Mustang. Ford, baby! Ford.

Not Interested: Is that a good car?

Interested: Damn right it's a good car.

Not Interested: I see.

Interested: Does your car go fast?

Not Interested: It goes however fast I make it go. Generally around forty miles an hour I guess.

Interested: Fuck that! My car goes 140 miles per hour. 140, baby! 140. That is one hundred more than yours goes.

Not Interested: Right.

[Long pause.]

Interested: I am thinking about getting some nitrous.

Not Interested: Some what?

Interested: Make my Mustang go like forty miles per hour faster. If I want it to.

Interested: Do you drive many places at 180 miles per hour?

[Long pause.]

Interested: Who do you think is taller, you or me?

Not Interested: I really have no idea.

Interested: I bet I am taller than you.

Not Interested: You're probably right.

Interested: You know how tall I am?

Not Interested: [Sighing] I don't know, five-ten, five-eleven?

Interested: More like six-one. I'm six-one, baby! Six-one.

Not interested: Okay.

Interested: How tall are you?

Not Interested: Five-nine or so.

Interested: That is what I thought.

Not Interested: You thought I was five-nine?

Interested: I don't know. All I know is I am three inches taller than you, baby.

Not Interested: Right.

(310 WORDS)

DISCUSSION

Do you think these two guys can ever find any common ground and, if so, what? Flip the exchange so that "Not Interested" is going on and on about what bores "Interested."

Ryan Ridge: "Shaky Hands & All"

I was an unemployed astrologer suffering from writer's block. The stars were bad and I refused to play middleman. Like so many of my fellow horoscope writers, I found myself chasing the narrative arc of daytime soaps with warm beer and cigarettes, intermittently ambling to the mailbox to fetch my unemployment stipend.

● ● ●

She was an out-of-work manicurist who'd been wrongfully accused of failing to wash her hands before returning from the bathroom. She quit

after union threats. She began reading palms. Career-wise it was prof-
itable, given the state of things.

● ● ●

We met in the lobby of the Psychic Job Fair, where she summoned me to
a little booth near the back of the auditorium. "Your palm reads like a
cheap romance novel," she said. She dropped my hand and asked what
I was doing later.

● ● ●

At her place, we drank Robitussin and played strip poker with a deck of
Tarot cards. In our skivvies, she gazed directly through my forehead and
said: "I see you inside me."
    One . . . two . . . three minutes later, I apologized. "Didn't see that
coming, did you?"
    "No, but I see you buying me breakfast."
    "Shake on it," I said.
    We reached out to shake hands, but they were already shaking.

(204 WORDS)

DISCUSSION

How does this double portrait add up to greater than one plus one?
What impels two people to get together, and what role does sex play?
Why does the whole process make people nervous?

Mass Compression

IF FLASH FICTION WORKS BY COMPRESSION, maybe you *can* fit an entire life into a page or two. Take a character from birth to death, or at least early years to dotage, in a few well-chosen paragraphs. It's the opposite of a vignette, in which a mere scene may represent a whole life. In mass compression, everything seems to occur at high speed: your first lost tooth, winning a soccer game, graduation from law school, your second child developing mumps, your second divorce, and retirement from the law firm of Atkins and Swift. That's it: it's over. Because of the speed at which the events pass by, the effect may be somewhat comic (think of the old days of silent movies, the action speeded up so that the actors look like automatons) or tragic (a whole existence, with all its highs and lows, reduced to five paragraphs).

Here are some tips:

Try syncope, a figurative term meaning the omission of the middle: a drink before and a cigarette after, to represent two people making love; two tense sentences sandwiching a bank robbery, the planning and the aftermath.

Go for synecdoche, part for whole: one short but memorable sum-up to represent each phase in the life of a failure. Start with a bungled breech delivery, leaving a forceps mark on his forehead; the father didn't just leave when the boy was two, but came back and left three more times before never returning; at school, the kid flunked math so many times that the teachers finally gave him a dishonorable discharge; and so on.

Go for details that really stand out. Think of what the cardinal events of a life are, but try to go beyond the ones that everyone else comes up with: birth, graduation, wedding, children, retirement, funeral. How about the time that you made a perfect score in the video game Razzle? The time that you ran out of gas seventy miles outside Reno?

Be proportionate. Draw upon all significant phases of life, from the awkward tween years to an assisted-living facility when your character's in her eighties. Now toss in a surprise event: winning the chili cook-off at age eighty-five, copyrighting the recipe, and making some real money from it.

Try for an arc of sorts or, if the life you construct hasn't got that shape, maybe some highs and lows. If you do include the mundane, show why it's there and how it fits into the story. Standing at the bus stop indicates a life of waiting.

Consider the what-ifs. Suppose the skateboard accident hadn't occurred, or she went to another party that night and never met Ian? Any regrets, victories? What else would have changed?

What does a life add up to, anyway? If art is life with the boring parts left out, good art adds up to more than the sum of its parts.

EXERCISES

❶ Determine what sort of character you'll be accompanying on his brief life (media mogul? track star?), then make a list of key incidents appropriate (or wickedly inappropriate) to that person's existence. Humor is always welcome, or at least outlandishness. The real trick is to make the ordinary come across as meaningful and emotionally resonant.

❷ In 500 words, tell the story of your entire family for the last three generations.

READINGS

Bruce Holland Rogers: "Dinosaur"

When he was very young, he waved his arms, snapped his massive jaws, and tromped around the house so that the dishes trembled in the china cabinet. "Oh, for goodness' sake," his mother said. "You are *not* a dinosaur! You are a human being!" Since he was not a dinosaur, he thought for a time that he might be a pirate. "Seriously," his father said to him after school one day, "what *do* you want to be?" A fireman, maybe. Or a policeman. Or a soldier. Some kind of hero.

But in high school they gave him tests and told him he was good with numbers. Perhaps he'd like to be a math teacher? That was respectable. Or a tax accountant? He could make a lot of money doing that. It seemed a good idea to make money, what with falling in love and thinking about raising a family. So he became a tax accountant, even though he sometimes regretted it, because it made him feel, well, small. And he felt even smaller when he was no longer a tax accountant, but a retired tax accountant. Still worse: a retired tax accountant who forgot things. He forgot to take the garbage to the curb, to take his pill, to turn his hearing aid on. Every day it seemed he forgot more things, important things, like where his children lived and which of them were married or divorced.

Then one day, when he was out for a walk by the lake, he forgot what his mother had told him. He forgot that he was not a dinosaur. He stood blinking his dinosaur eyes in the bright sunlight, feeling its familiar warmth on his dinosaur skin, watching dragonflies flitting among the horsetails at the water's edge.

(293 WORDS)

DISCUSSION

What's left out of this story? Add five facts that really add to the whole.

Susan O'Neill: "Memento Mori"

The baby was born with a hole in her spine, and all the love that Estelle and Art poured into it was not enough to seal her tiny soul inside. Estelle—daughter of Florida, tall, thin and elegant—chain-smoked cigarettes in a silver holder and clung to Art's broad chest. She swallowed her grief, buried it in her vacant womb, polished it to a fist-sized pearl with unshed tears. A year later, it thrust itself into the surgeon's hand, leaving her barren.

I was born then, Art's sister's first girl. Baby-simple, I warmed to my aunt's caresses, not knowing I had stolen them.

Estelle and Art lived exotic in the brick jungle of Chicago, while I tended cows and schoolbooks. I saw them little. But in my tenth summer, they drove me with them to Florida. My mother said, "You have always been her favorite."

I cared nothing for the Why. Wild with ocean, shoes leaking sand, I body-surfed breakers and gobbled crayfish, and gaped as Estelle's tiny mother dipped snuff from a jeweled snap-top box. I filled my Brownie camera with wonders: segregated beaches, motels. Tobacco fields. Lookout Mountain. Art and Estelle; her regal poise; his frayed black stogies. Leaning on the Buick. His broad hand brown on her lady-white shoulders. Her bobbed black hair against his muscled arm.

Summer died. I stumbled fiercely about the barn, kicking chickens, stabbing cows with truculent stares.

For Art, winter brought death. Mother told me one wind-whipped school afternoon: his heart.

I felt loss. But I was selfishly young, filled with books and plans and, yes, the dreaded cows. Estelle pulled Art's old Buick up to the snow-bound house. Her head high, she drew me to her narrow smoky bosom, laid a scarlet-tipped finger on my cheek and searched my eyes—for what, I did not know. Then she nodded and drove away. To replant herself in Florida, with her mother.

I grew away, fast-forwarding from farm and family, grew like Jack's beanstalk through clouds into a blue sky of airplanes, into far-flung agoras and feluccas and minarets and yurts. I fell in love in a jungle, far from cows; we shimmered with life and purpose and made perfect children.

In Florida, a past land. Estelle's mother shrank and faded away. I sent the obligatory letter; I received pictures—Estelle tall, pole-thin, rail-straight, long cigarette held split-fingered at her chin, now minus the holder. Alone. Old. In her new Buick. Her letter spoke, strangely, of Art: Ah, I miss the man. He knew me.

She was eighty when her smoke-brittled bones crumbled. Estelle was gone, drifted ash, before I reached Florida. Side by side, my mother and I boxed away chic size-two dresses for charity in her haunted, orderly house.

In a bedroom redolent of pine and old smoke, buried deep beneath sweaters and lavender sachet, I found a small snow-white box.

Inside, cradled lovingly in rose-dotted tissue, lay hand-knit pink baby booties.

(491 WORDS)

DISCUSSION

What is the narrator like, inherent in what specifics? What details does fast-forwarding blur, and which does it highlight? How could you alter that emphasis?

Metafiction

METAFICTION IS WRITING ABOUT WRITING, self-reflexive and self-conscious. If the aim of regular fiction is to create the appearance of reality, metafiction attempts to shatter that illusion, to show the audience
that this is art, not life. In a conventional story, we read about a man
named Ned and his troubles with his ex-wife, Heather. The dialogue
sounds real, and the plot, about an impending child-support lawsuit,
compelling. But in the middle of a bitter exchange between Ned and
Heather about who earns more money, the narrative stops. "Listen,"
says Ned, "you don't really believe in this setup, do you?"

"Yeah," chimes in Heather, "we're just a bunch of words that the
author strung together."

In drama, this violation of verisimilitude is called breaking the
fourth wall. Playwrights like Bertolt Brecht and Tom Stoppard excel
at it. But it's also been done to perfection by fiction writers like John
Barth and Donald Barthelme. In flash fiction, you'll probably have time
for just a setup and an exposé, a point registered. Think of a comic strip
character in frame four, looking upward and noticing that his world is
bound by horizontal and vertical black lines.

"What's the point?" you may ask. (Are you real or just my imaginary audience?) The sheer novelty effect for some readers is enough. It

may also function as a commentary on life and art and the pathetic attempts of one to imitate the other. Imagine the usual shoot-out about to happen in a western, when suddenly the tall gunslinger throws down his Colt .45 and snarls, "I'm tired of these stereotypes! If this writer can't rig up something fresher, I'm not gonna shoot."

"I'm with you," says the guy wearing the fringed vest. "Next thing you know, we'll be walking into the saloon with the swinging doors and asking for a shot of rotgut." (See the "Genre" chapter on avoiding these kinds of clichés.)

Metafiction can bring an awareness of writing's limits and limitations or its boundaries and its drawbacks. Because it dispenses with fictional conventions, it can also say and do things that you can't say and do in regular stories. Imagine a flash fiction in which two characters comment on their weaknesses as girlfriends. They'd never do that in real life—they'd be far too self-conscious—but this is metafiction, and in fact they end up remarking on the author's shortcomings in that area. Wait, here comes the kicker: the final line is a comment about you, the reader.

Metafiction can be fun, like a game with new rules or one whose rules you're making up as you go. But be advised:

A lot of metafiction has already been written, so don't just repeat the usual patterns: this character (surprise!) starts talking back to her creator.

Don't engage in metafiction just because you can't think of anything else to write about, like the rookie blogger who starts blogging *about* her blog in week five. In fiction workshops, this is the student who couldn't come up with a story, so that's what his narrative's about.

Must your protagonists always be writers? Maybe it's time to look out the window instead of in the mirror. Your protagonist doesn't always have to be a reflection of yourself.

EXERCISES

❶ Find a piece of flash fiction you like and expose its underpinnings through the characters' dialogue: how they think the author came up with the idea, the people, and the events. Have the characters try to improve their situation.

❷ Fictionalize yourself; that is, turn yourself into a character. Do it differently in two takes, and, in the third take, have the two characters argue about which image is superior.

READINGS

Ptim Callan: "Story"

This is an outsourced text. The authorial voice known (or, for the most part, unknown) as Ptim Callan has outsourced the creation of this short story to a multinational contracting agency whose name could not appropriately—tastefully—be given here. Ptim Callan determined that his to-date successes have been more in the line of business and less in the line of fictioneering. Testifying to his habit as a successful businessman, Callan decided to further specialize, to outsource his less successful endeavors in favor of the more successful ones. Just as a corporation learns to distinguish a sustainable core competency from an expendable resource drain, so has Callan. In his work life Callan removed employees from unnecessary areas, allowing outsource agencies to perform these same tasks. Manufacturers, creative agencies, development labs, all these organizations could better serve the needs of Callan's corporate employer than its own human and capital resources were.

Callan has pursued this same strategy to a lesser degree for years. He pays a housekeeper and a gardener and a tax accountant and a financial consultant. All these experts are examples of individual specialization, of a person recognizing where his strengths lie and where the investment of dollars in an employee will go further than investment of his own time and need to learn. But the real masterstroke was to apply these same principles to all aspects of his personal life. Now Callan has a professional driver to take his car out on weekends, a charming guy who dates women on his behalf, and a nice fellow who calls his mother. This piece was generated by a slave-wage ghostwriter whose talent for writing outclasses his talent for business as Callan's for business does his for writing. We hope you have enjoyed this piece. After all, Ptim Callan paid top dollar for it.

(301 WORDS)

DISCUSSION

What kind of person is the speaker? Is anything the matter with his logic? Would you trust your writing to be executed by someone else—or write for someone like this speaker?

Jorge Luis Borges: "Borges and I"
TRANSLATED BY ANDREW HURLEY

It's Borges, the other one, that things happen to. I walk through Buenos Aires and I pause—mechanically now, perhaps—to gaze at the arch of an entryway and its inner door; news of Borges reaches me by mail, or I see his name on a list of academics or in some biographical dictionary. My taste runs to hourglasses, maps, seventeenth-century typefaces, etymologies, the taste of coffee, and the prose of Robert Louis Stevenson; Borges shares these preferences, but in a vain sort of way that turns them into the accoutrements of an actor. It would be an exaggeration to say that our relationship is hostile—I live, I allow myself to live, so that Borges can spin out his literature, and that literature is my justification. I willingly admit that he has written a number of sound pages, but those pages will not save *me*, perhaps because the good in them no longer belongs to any individual, not even to that other man, but rather to language itself, or to tradition. Beyond that, I am doomed—utterly and inevitably—to oblivion, and fleeting moments will be all of me that survives in that other man. Little by little, I have been turning

everything over to him, though I know the perverse way he has of dis-
torting and magnifying everything. Spinoza believed that all things wish
to go on being what they are—stone wishes eternally to be stone, and
tiger, to be tiger. I shall endure in Borges, not in myself (if, indeed, I am
anybody at all), but I recognize myself less in his books than in many
others', or in the tedious strumming of a guitar. Years ago I tried to free
myself from him, and I moved on from the mythologies of the slums and
outskirts of the city to games with time and infinity, but those games
belong to Borges now, and I shall have to think up other things. So my
life is a point-counterpoint, a kind of fugue, and a falling away—and
everything winds up being lost to me, and everything falls into oblivion,
or into the hands of the other man.

I am not sure which of us it is that's writing this page.

(365 WORDS)

DISCUSSION

What's a writer when not writing? Do you write to express yourself,
compensate for perceived deficiencies, or just for amusement?

Vanishing Point

IF FLASH FICTION WORKS BY OMISSION, compression, and concentration, what happens in even shorter forms? In fact, the original term *flash fiction*, dating back to the early 1990s, referred to something shorter than short-shorts (which might extend for five or six pages). Flash fiction was to be read in a flash. Also, many short narratives, particularly in earlier eras, are brief simply because that's all the space their narratives demand. Flash fiction, on the other hand, was an art form deliberately crafted to fit into a certain space, often 500 to 1,000 words. The pieces in *Flash Fiction: 72 Very Short Stories*, which came out in 1992, showcase this form well: not "this is how long it took me to wrap it up," but "look what I can do in a page or two." Finally: the original flash fiction, because it was based on the word *flash*, connoted speed and dazzle. A webzine called *SmokeLong Quarterly* got its title because the work it prints takes as much time to read as it takes to smoke a cigarette. Whatever this briefer form accomplishes is up to you. However, here are a few pointers:

1   Hit the ground running. No time for polite introductions (or throat-clearing conclusions). Thrust the reader right into a situation—Keneesha is drowning in the middle of the lake—and keep the scene moving.

2 Learn to develop on several fronts at once. "Dizzy from ten tabs of Percodan, Keneesha can only watch her arms and legs flail uselessly" both progresses the action and develops the character.

3 Save space for cool imagery. Keneesha is disappearing under the surface like a bee trapped in a blossom. The water, so inviting a moment ago, has become a thirty-foot-deep enemy.

4 Do more with less. If short-shorts tend to reside in a scene, really short flash fiction may focus on a moment: the two minutes in which Keneesha Hughes becomes no more.

5 [In the interests of brevity, point 5 has been omitted. Come up with your own.]

Microfiction, a term in vogue since Jerome Stern's anthology *Micro Fiction* in 1996, may be more lyrical and static than flash fiction. As with any of these terms, the definition may be somewhat fluid, but the suggested length limit is 250 words. Many microfiction pieces feature simply an encounter or a realization: a school principal talking to a janitor, or a man coming to terms with his earlier self.

Of course, once the popularity of truly short fiction became established, writers wanted to push the edge of the envelope. In America, you can make a reputation by taking almost any object and making it either much bigger or much smaller. Hence was born hint fiction, an entire narrative in 25 words or fewer. Here's an example by Merrilee Faber, from *Hint Fiction: Stories in 25 Words or Fewer*, edited by Robert Swartwood and Natalie McNabb: "We came around the corner, and there they were: young lovers, hands clasped. I drew the outline, Joe directed the crowd."

It's called "Love Is Forever."

Intimidated? Here's what you can do:

1 Limn [good word] a situation. Mom needs to cook dinner, but the stove is gone. Or try a setup. Charlie's about to sneeze, but if he does, the world will come to an end.

2 Turn in a small space. Go for irony, a twist, or a payoff of some kind. Phil's best friend is his clone. Phil is a turtle.

Or brilliantly turn against these guidelines and create a mini-masterpiece that floats in space and remains vivid in readers' minds for years. If you don't try again and again, you'll never know whether you could have done it.

Nanofiction, also known as Twitter fiction, is another recent form. The social medium Twitter started up in 2006 with a limit of 140 characters for each post, including spaces between words. Though its space limit may still seem daunting, people have tweeted everything from breaking news to recipes, anecdotes, and PR releases. Inevitably, people started tweeting fiction. (It used to be that if you wanted the piece to be retweeted, you'd have to keep it as short as 120 characters so that people could add hashtags to the end.) The site Nanoism, started by Ben White, dates back to 2009. It tends toward the satiric and the grotesque:

> It was pretending to be his wife again; two feet on the stairs, the other six on the walls. "Come out, Ben. Please!" It did her voice too.
>
> — DEAN CLAYTON EDWARDS

> She raised the glass and downed the love potion.
> Soon, she would love him back.
>
> — DAVIAN AW

In 2012, the British newspaper the *Guardian* posted "Twitter Fiction: 21 Authors Try Their Hands at 140-Character Novels," with results by novelists ranging from David Lodge to A. M. Holmes. Some writers have also attempted serialized stories via tweets, but the results don't always fit into even flash fiction space constraints.

In any event, nanofiction isn't exclusively a cyber-age phenomenon. Read—or witness—"The Dinosaur," by the Spanish author Augusto Monterroso, published in 1959 and translated by Edith Grossman:

> When he awoke, the dinosaur was still there.

Here are some tips for writing nanofiction:

1 Variations on a theme: if you build on a known context, such as Little Red Riding Hood, you need only a few words to tie into a full-length narrative, or a news story that everyone remembers years later. Remember the Alamo.

2 Punch lines or other well-known tags may evoke material without retelling the whole story. "To get to the other side" puts people in mind of the question "Why did the chicken cross the road?"

3 Try weird conditions with the implications left to suggestion. Since a lot of odd premises have been played and replayed, try a familiar one in a different direction. If you study really hard, you'll do well on the physics exam—unless something far more important grabs your attention during the test.

Where can you go from here? The world will end in a minute from now. What will you do in that time? Write your answer in no more than 140 characters.

The Future

YEARS AGO, the ambition of most short story writers was to appear in print, preferably in a literary journal or magazine. With a high-circulation magazine like *The New Yorker*, you could count on a large audience, with readers of all stripes. With a literary quarterly like *The Paris Review*, you had the ear of the literati or the intelligentsia, a smaller group than a high-circulation readership but often aligned politically or aesthetically.

Print has fallen on hard times, with newspapers and magazines suffering declines in circulation and advertising. Many have gone out of business; some have gravitated to the Web, where the production costs are far lower. And though the reading experience on the old computer screens was a real issue, e-readers (what a quaint term that will seem one day!) are now everywhere. What difference does it make whether someone reads your flash fiction on some stapled-together pages or on a gray half-scale screen? Electronic readers can also provide what most books can't: sound and graphics. Not smell, taste, or touch, but see the revised 30th anniversary edition of this textbook for an update in this area. They can also provide connections to other material, such as five cool links to carnival face painting, a network of associations rather than a few references in a paragraph.

What does this mean for your short fiction? The Web has a way of expanding possibilities and bending forms. If your piece is online, it can pull in multimedia, including mind-bending graphics. When describing how your characters' grandparents are apes, cut to a Wiki pic of a bonobo. And don't restrict yourself to just images: think of sounds, not just music, like the opening of Beethoven's Fifth Symphony but also the echo of someone yelling in a 500-foot-wide canyon.

Make your readers aware of what's out there. You can also reach more viewers, potentially, than you can if you appear in issue #1 of *Yellow Dragonfly Review* (apologies to the editor of *YDR*, which I hope makes it to issue #2). A lot of people out there are writing online, which makes for a crowded arena, but new ideas seem to create their own space. If 299,999,999 ideas have been taken, there's always the 300,000,000th. Cultivate an idiosyncratic viewpoint—you're you, after all. How about a flash fiction that showcases an ugly divorce but with you as the 2010 Subaru Legacy that gets fought over? At the end, cut to a video of a Subaru driving down I-95.

Another direction to go in is hypertext, one of the earlier forms of interactive narrative. Michael Joyce's 1987 story "afternoon," in which a father looks for a son who may have been injured in an accident, is a well-known example. As the story proceeds, it offers choices for the reader to click, a branching set of narrative possibilities. Computer users from the late 1970s may remember Colossal Cave Adventure, also known as Advent, an adventure game designed by the computer programmer Will Crowther, with lines like "YOU ARE INSIDE A BUILDING, A WELL HOUSE FOR A LARGE SPRING. THERE ARE SOME KEYS ON THE GROUND HERE. THERE IS A SHINY BRASS LAMP NEARBY. THERE IS FOOD HERE. THERE IS A BOTTLE OF WATER HERE." And so forth. The type of adventure you had depended on what you chose to explore and which objects you chose to take with you. Some children's game books, such as the Choose Your Own Adventure series, work similarly by directing readers to different pages based on choices they make.

Whether or not you like participating that way as a reader, hypertext makes a good point: why should the reader be passive rather than participate in the creation of the text? The writer has created the world and its available options, but it changes depending on what's chosen. Actions have consequences.

How can you apply that to flash fiction? What looks like a flow-chart on the page becomes a hypertext onscreen. The woman shoots at an elephant. If she hits it, she angers the whole tribe, who regard the elephant as sacred. If she misses, the elephant charges and injures her. If the tribe gets angry at her, she either attempts to talk to them or else tries to outrun them. If the elephant charges and injures her, she either breaks her arm or else sprains her wrist. End by having her leave Africa. Or staying and becoming part of the tribe. Or . . .

The hypertext may also appear as paragraphs with certain words highlighted as links, which lead to other paragraphs when clicked on. In 2009, the writer Susan Gibbs composed "100 Hypertext Flash Fictions" in this fashion, available at Hypercompendia.

For truly short pieces, you might want to reduce the flow-chart narrative to one choice or a story with two possible endings. You can accomplish this effect solely in print, though it may not look as neat.

Other possibilities? Consider fan fiction based on a well-known TV show or Netflix series or graphic novel or anime—but flash-fiction size, merely an outtake or a scene. You could crowd-source the sentences. You could even use bot-written texts, algorithm-based programs adhering to some basic narrative patterns that you input.

How novel is all this? New and not new. "What has been is what will be, and what has been done is what will be done, and there is nothing new under the sun" (only 114 characters, from Ecclesiastes in the English Standard Version of the Bible). But don't be discouraged. You can always find a new angle or two.

EXERCISES

❶ What do tigers, princesses, and marriage have in common? Provide Web links to show some connections, and base a story on them.

❷ Write a 500-word hypertext flash fiction about a character who's clumsy. Each time she drop something or bumps into someone, the result can be either bad or good. Provide an ending that stops all further choices, though it needn't be death.

READINGS

Flash fiction in hypertext is in scarce supply, as is multimedia flash fiction. Fill that gap. Make sure that your links or added media really add dimensions, not just background.

Conclusion

IF YOU'VE COME THIS FAR WITHOUT SKIPPING SECTIONS, you've progressed through a gamut of flash fiction forms, from prose poems and vignettes to twist stories and metafiction. You've studied technique, application, and examples. You've also absorbed many lessons in compression. But you should still read more. And more. We all should. Following this section is a list of anthologies, publishers, zines, and websites you might want to check out, incomplete and a bit inaccurate because it was compiled on Monday, and today is Tuesday. Matters change fast in this realm. And though it was tempting to include single-author flash fiction collections, there are too many these days for such an attempt, and the matter of inclusion and omission would result in far too many close judgment calls and hard feelings. Let's just say there's a great deal of good work being published that all curious readers should explore.

Bibliography

BOOKS

Asimov, Isaac, and Groff Conklin, eds. *50 Short Science Fiction Tales*. New York: Collier Books, 1963.

Beckel, Abigail, and Kathleen Rooney, eds. *Brevity and Echo: An Anthology of Short Short Stories*. Brookline, MA: Rose Metal Press, 2006.

Brown, Randall. *A Pocket Guide to Flash Fiction*. Wynnewood, PA: Matter Press, 2012.

Butler, Robert Olen, ed. *The Best Small Fictions, 2015*. Plano, TX: Queen's Ferry Press, 2015.

Gingher, Marianne, ed. *Long Story Short: Flash Fiction by Sixty-Five of North Carolina's Finest Writers*. Chapel Hill: University of North Carolina Press, 2009.

Hazuka, Tom, ed. *Flash Fiction Funny: 82 Very Short Humorous Stories*. New York: Blue Light Press, 2013.

Hazuka, Tom, and Mark Budman, eds. *You Have Time for This: Contemporary American Short-Short Stories*. New York: Ooligan Press, 2007.

Hazuka, Tom, Denise Thomas, and James Thomas, eds. *Flash Fiction: 72 Very Short Stories*. New York: Norton, 1992.

Howe, Irving, and Ilana Wiener Howe, eds. *Short Shorts: An Anthology of the Shortest Stories*. Boston: David R. Godine, 1982.

Marsh, Tara L., ed. *The Rose Metal Press Field Guide to Writing Flash Fiction: Tips from Editors, Teachers, and Writers in the Field*. Rose Metal Press, 2013.

Michel, Lincoln, and Nadxieli Nieto, eds. *Gigantic Worlds*. New York: Gigantic Books, 2015.

Monaghan, Nicole, ed. *Stripped: A Collection of Anonymous Flash Fiction*. Philadelphia, PA: PS Books, 2011.

Moore, Dinty, ed. *Sudden Stories: The MAMMOTH Book of Miniscule Fiction*. Dubois, PA: MAMMOTH, 2003.

Perkins-Hazuka, Christine, Tom Hazuka, and Mark Budman, eds. *Sudden Flash Youth: 65 Short-Short Stories*. New York: Persea, 2011.

Richmond, Michelle, ed. *Flash in the Attic: 33 Very Short Stories*. Flash in the Attic Flash Fiction Anthology, vol. 1. New York: Fiction Attic Press, 2013.

Shapard, Robert, and James Thomas, eds. *Flash Fiction Forward: 80 Very Short Stories*. New York: Norton, 2006.

Shapard, Robert, and James Thomas, eds. *New Sudden Fiction: Short-Short Studies from America and Beyond*. New York: Norton, 2007.

Shapard, Robert, and James Thomas, eds. *Sudden Fiction: American Short-Short Stories*. Layton, UT: Gibbs Smith, 1986.

Shapard, Robert, and James Thomas, eds. *Sudden Fiction, Continued: 60 New Short-Short Stories*. New York: Norton, 1996.

Shapard, Robert, and James Thomas, eds. *Sudden Fiction International: 60 Short-Short Stories*. New York: Norton, 1989.

Shapard, Robert, and James Thomas, eds. *Sudden Fiction Latino: Short Stories from the United States and Latin America*. New York: Norton, 2010.

Stern, Jerome, ed. *Micro Fiction: An Anthology of 50 Really Short Stories*. New York: Norton, 1996.

Swartwood, Robert, ed. *Hint Fiction: An Anthology of Stories in 25 Words or Fewer*. New York: Norton, 2010.

Thomas, James, Robert Shapard, and Christopher Merrill, eds. *Flash Fiction International: Very Short Stories from Around the World*. New York: Norton, 2015.

Ziegler, Alan, ed. *Short: An International Anthology of Five Centuries of Short-Short Stories, Prose Poems, Brief Essays, and Other Short Prose Forms*. New York: Persea, 2014.

PUBLISHERS

Hobart

Matter Press

Queen's Ferry Press
Rose Metal Press

ZINES AND WEBSITES

Best of the Net
Corium Magazine
Flash Fiction Chronicles
Flashfiction.net
Flash Fiction Online
The Journal of Compressed Creative Arts
matchbook
Microfiction Monday
Nanoism
100 Word Story
101 Words
Sixwordstories.net/
SmokeLong Quarterly
Wigleaf

Note: two-sentence horror stories and variations on that idea are available on many websites.

Second note: given the evanescence of the Web, some of these listings may already have passed into limbo, to be replaced by others.

Permissions

ANONYMOUS: "Two monks" (the story of Tanzan and Ekido). From *An Introduction to Literature*, 9th ed., edited by Sylvan Barnet, Morton Berman, and William Burto (Glenview, IL: Scott Foresman, 1989). Reprinted by permission of Sylvan Barnet.

DAVIAN AW: "She raised the glass and downed the love potion." From *Nanoism*. Reprinted by permission of the author.

ISAAC BABEL: "An Incident on the Nevsky Prospekt," translated by Peter Constantine. From *The Complete Works of Isaac Babel* (New York: Norton, 2002). Reprinted by permission of W. W. Norton & Company.

DONALD BARTHELME: "The Baby." From *Overnight to Many Distant Cities* (New York: Putnam, 1983). Reprinted by permission of the Wylie Agency.

JORGE LUIS BORGES: "Borges and I," translated by Andrew Hurley. From *Collected Fictions* (New York: Viking, 1998). Reprinted by permission of the Wylie Agency, Penguin USA, Penguin Canada, and Penguin UK.

RICHARD BRAUTIGAN: "A Need for Gardens." From *Revenge of the Lawn* (New York: Touchstone, 1971). Reprinted by permission of Sarah Lazin Books.

MARK BUDMAN: "The Diary of a Salaryman." From *You Have Time for This*, edited by Mark Budman and Tom Hazuka (Portland, OR: Ooligan Press, 2007). Reprinted by permission of the author.

CHRISTINE BYL: "Hey, Jess McCafferty." From *Sudden Flash Youth*, edited by Christine Perkins-Hazuka, Mark Budman, and Tom Hazuka (New York: Persea, 2011). Reprinted by permission of the author.

PTIM CALLAN: "Story." From *42Opus* 3, no. 3 (September 2003). Reprinted by permission of the author.

COLETTE: "The Other Wife," translated by Matthew Ward. From *The Collected Stories of Colette* (New York: Farrar, Straus and Giroux, 1984). Reprinted by permission of Farrar, Straus and Giroux.

JOHN COLLIER: "The Chaser." From *Fancies and Goodnights* (Garden City, NY: Doubleday, 1951). Reprinted by permission of the Harold Matson Company, Inc.

RAPHAEL DAGOLD: "The Two Rats and the BB Gun." From *Quarterly West* (Spring/Summer 2001), reprinted in *Sudden Flash Youth*, edited by Christine Perkins-Hazuka, Mark Budman, and Tom Hazuka (New York: Persea, 2011). Reprinted by permission of the author.

DEAN CLAYTON EDWARDS: "It was pretending to be his wife again." From *Nanoism*. Reprinted by permission of the author.

JOSEFINA ESTRADA: "The Extravagant Behavior of the Naked Woman," translated by Margaret Jull Costa. From *Flash Fiction International: Very Short Stories from Around the World*, edited by Robert Shapard and James Thomas (New York: Norton, 2015).

MERRILEE FABER: "Love Is Forever." From *Hint Fiction: An Anthology of Stories in 25 Words or Fewer*, edited by Robert Swartwood (New York: Norton, 2010). Reprinted by permission of the author.

ROXANE GAY: "The Mistress of Baby Breath." From *Reflection's Edge* 10 (2009). Reprinted by permission of the author.

WAYLAND HILTON-YOUNG: "The Choice." From *Punch* (1952). Reprinted by permission of Punch Limited.

PHIL KARASIK: "Mickey the Dog Phones Home." From *McSweeney's Internet Tendency*. Reprinted by permission of the author.

YASUNARI KAWABATA: "Canaries," translated by J. Martin Holman. From *Palm-of-the-Hand Stories* (New York: North Point Press, 1990). Reprinted by permission of Farrar, Straus and Giroux.

YUSEF KOMUNYAKAA: "Nude Interrogation." From *Thieves of Paradise* (Middletown, CT: Wesleyan University Press, 1998). Reprinted by permission of Wesleyan University Press.

LEN KUNTZ: "Story Problems." From *Eunoia Review*, January 7, 2011. Reprinted by permission of the author.

L. E. LEONE: "The Argument for a Shotgun." From *You Have Time for This*, edited by Mark Budman and Tom Hazuka Portland, OR: Ooligan Press, 2007). Reprinted by permission of the author.

STEVE MARTIN: "Disgruntled Former Lexicographer." From *The New Yorker*, October 11, 1999. Reprinted by permission of ICM Partners.

AUGUSTO MONTERROSO: "The Dinosaur," translated by Edith Grossman. From *Complete Works and Other Stories* (Austin: University of Texas Press, 1995). Reprinted by permission of the University of Texas Press.

BHARATI MUKHERJEE: "Courtly Vision." From *Darkness* (New York: Penguin, 1985). Reprinted by permission of Janklow & Nesbit Associates.

DICKY MURPHY: "The Magician's Umbrella." From *Lady Churchill's Rosebud Wristlet* 24 (2009). Reprinted by permission of the author.

SUSAN O'NEILL: "Memento Mori." From *You Have Time for This*, edited by Mark Budman and Tom Hazuka (Portland, OR: Ooligan Press, 2007). Reprinted by permission of the author.

TARA ORCHARD: "My Love." Reprinted by permission of the author.

RYAN RIDGE: "Shaky Hands & All." From *Flash Fiction Funny*, edited by Tom Hazuka (San Francisco: Blue Light Press, 2013); reprinted in *Hunters and Gamblers*, by Ryan Ridge (Ann Arbor, Mich.: Dzanc Books, 2013). Reprinted by permission of the author.

BRUCE HOLLAND ROGERS: "Dinosaur." Reprinted by permission of the author.

SAKI (HECTOR HUGH MUNRO): "The Open Window." From *Beasts and Super Beasts* (London: John Lane, 1914).

ROBERT SCHIPITS: "Dialogue Between Two Teenagers, One Interested in Cars and One Not." From *McSweeney's Internet Tendency*. Reprinted by permission of the author.

SEI SHŌNAGON: "Annoying Things." From *The Pillow Book of Sei Shōnagon*, translated by Ivan Morris (New York: Columbia University Press, 1991). Reprinted by permission of Columbia University Press.

WILL STANTON: "Barney." From *The Magazine of Fantasy and Science Fiction* (February 1951). Reprinted by permission of Linda Stanton-French.

BRUCE TAYLOR: "Exercise." From *Vestal Review* (2001). Reprinted by permission of the author.

LUISA VALENZUELA: "Vision Out of the Corner of One Eye," translated by Helen Lane. Reprinted by permission of the author.

ALICE WALKER: "The Flowers." From *In Love and Trouble* (New York: Harvest-Harcourt, 1973). Reprinted by permission of Houghton Mifflin Harcourt and the Joy Harris Literary Agency.

JEFFREY WHITMORE: "Bedtime Story." From *The World's Shortest Stories*, edited by Steve Moss (San Luis Obispo, CA: New Times Press, 1995). Reprinted by permission of Running Press and the author.

JOHN EDGAR WIDEMAN: "Witness." From *Serving House: A Journal of Literary Arts* 9 (Spring 2014). Reprinted by permission of the Wylie Agency.

Index

CPSIA information can be obtained
at www.ICGtesting.com
Printed in the USA
LVHW011218030319
609304LV00015B/742